A Mediator's Musings

*on Mediation, Negotiation, Politics
and a Changing World*

Volume 2

John Sturrock

Please write to:

Core Solutions
Scott House
10 South St Andrew Street
Edinburgh
EH2 2AZ
enquiries@core-solutions.com

John's blogs are published on:

www.core-solutions.com

Cover and text design by Ainsley Francis

www.ainsleyfrancis.com

Contents

The Climate Emergency – and Mediation . 75

The War in Ukraine - and Peace-Making . 93

Introduction

When I published *A Mediator's Musings* back in June 2020 (still available on Amazon!), we had only recently begun what turned out to be the first of a series of lockdowns as the COVID pandemic started to wreak its havoc. How the world seems to have changed since then, in so many ways.

The existential threat of climate change appears to have grown significantly and more quickly than many had predicted. The consequences are being felt more than ever before. The war in Ukraine, exacerbating the cost-of-living crisis, presents us with further threats of disruption and turmoil, possibly unlike anything we have faced for many years.

Politics and the state of public discourse continue to become more confrontational and abusive. And, in my own world of mediation and problem-solving, or peace-making, we face the age-old struggle to achieve real breakthroughs in acceptance that there are other and, many of us would argue, better ways than adversarial confrontation to resolve disputes and differences.

I mentioned in the Introduction to A Mediator's Musings that I hoped to write a "proper book". That remains my challenge. Now, as then, this second compilation of recent articles and blogs, with a few minor revisions, is an attempt to share my thinking, arranged according to some of the themes I mention above, and to be dipped into perhaps, rather than digested in one sitting. I have retained the article headings as published in the press, even though some may not have been quite what I would have chosen myself...

My thanks to my good friend, Dr Anna Howard, for her meticulous review and editing of a draft of this book.

And to my colleague, Emma Anstead, for also reading over the text and making many helpful suggestions. Finally, as ever, I am grateful for all the support my wife, Fiona, gives me as I pursue my journey. It is truly a joint venture!

John Sturrock
Edinburgh
October 2022

All proceeds from this book will go to aid research into strokes, from one of which I suffered in May 2021. I am grateful to say I have made a fairly full recovery but many are not so fortunate.

General Reflections – and Mediation

It is such a privilege to be able to write about a variety of topics and to have these observations published. Here is a selection from recent years of a more general nature, while often touching on mediation.

Reflecting on Purpose

The process of discerning what to write about in an article or a blog can be challenging. Sometimes inspiration comes quickly. On other occasions, there is a barren wilderness, or a hotchpotch of half-formed ideas.

This feels like the last of these. I thought to write about a really excellent new book by the Oxford economists, Paul Collier and John Kay, entitled *Greed is Dead, Politics after Individualism*. The authors distinguish *"authoritarian or contractual hierarchy"* (where instructions are cascaded down from the top) with *"mediating hierarchy"* involving *"constant negotiation"*; they criticise binary processes and outcomes as detrimental to the community; they comment that *"when disputes arise, they need to be resolved through processes which are accessible and inexpensive, and which search for compromise"*; and observe that *"collective intelligence is the combined product of competition and cooperation"*. Collier recently praised the work of mediators in an article in the New Statesman magazine. Much to ponder there.

Then there is the latest book by my good friend, the author, ecologist and scholar Alastair McIntosh, *Riders on the Storm*, at the same time one of the best summaries of the current science on climate change and associated environmental issues, and a timely challenge to each of us about needless consumption and escalating population – and, crucially, about the inner psychological and spiritual work which will be needed by all of us if we are to navigate the times ahead.

For mediators, it would be hard to look past a recent piece in Mediate. com by Ken Cloke (entitled The 2020 Elections, Mediation and the Political Divide – What Next?) with his usual insights into the role mediators can play in an evermore polarising world. This sentence alone gives much to consider: *"It is important ... to recognize that there are lower and higher forms of connection, cooperation, and common ground."* *"The lower form can be found in compromise...To reach higher common ground, it is necessary to affirm the common humanity of both parties."* Discuss!

However, I find it impossible to ignore an email I received recently from my good friend in Oregon, Tim Hicks, author of that outstanding book about the neural working of the brain and conflict, *Embodied*

Conflict: The Neural Basis of Conflict and Communication.

In response to an email to Tim to offer my concerns about the situation in Oregon, Tim replied in these terms, which I share with his permission:

"Thanks for your message. The past week has been exceptional. For us, personally, the impact has been staying indoors to avoid, as much as possible, the seriously hazardous smoke conditions. Visibility a couple of days ago was down to 100 yards. We've not seen the sun for days now. A fine and dangerous ash covers everything. The birds and other creatures are quieted. But many, as you know, have suffered far worse and continue to suffer. The large fire near us was about 25 miles away and was approaching in our direction for a couple of days before its advance slowed. There was one day we considered whether we might have to evacuate. Fortunately, we were spared. It was sobering to consider what to bring and the prospect of losing one's home to fire was stark.

All this is prelude, is it not. I've read predictions that multiple concurrent events will be the future's norm. I fear for our children and grandchildren. At one point, systems will begin to collapse (and psychologies along with them) and living may become much more chaotic and harsh.

I'm finding it difficult to be optimistic these days, and particularly because of the condition of social discourse in this country and the apparent unmooring of understanding from any kind of grounding in reality. There is something deeply saddening in the fracturing of this society's ability to rely on some level of reality consensus. The expansion of conspiracy theories and the number of people susceptible to them is like a kind of spreading miasma of psychosis, a deep and oppressive social fog in which people are stumbling around with no ability to agree on basic truths and understandings. Disagreements now are not founded on a basis of basic reality agreements but involve the very foundations of our reality constructing.

Though I am not feeling very optimistic and optimism is almost beginning to feel delusional, nevertheless, I appreciate the spirit of persistence and commitment to standing up and not giving up, regardless. As they say, better to go down fighting."

I don't think any message has so profoundly affected me in recent times as this from Tim. It reinforces for me how extraordinary are the times in which we live and the challenges we face individually and collectively – and globally. It is easy to forget, as the Western world experiences these dislocations, that many in the developing world have been facing such tragedies on a daily basis for years – and are much less well placed to cope with them.

Tim's message has caused me to ask again: **what should I be doing?**

It is so easy just to continue in the usual way, with the usual pursuits, finding comfort in the notion that there is not much that I, as a mere individual, can do. Or indeed to reassure myself, rather smugly, that at least what I am doing is "good work."

However, I conclude that this is not enough. I need a set of principles to guide my use of what will always be limited time, a set of criteria by which to guide my decisions about what initiatives or requests I should engage with – and how. Here is what I think I need to try and do:

- Put relationships first; without that, everything else will be less easy to manage and potentially damaging to me and others;
- Somehow, be kind and compassionate in all of these relationships – that will take discipline, especially when under pressure;
- Find appropriate time for my family and neighbours, those close to me through physical and psychological proximity;

- Consider the impact on the environment of everything I choose to do;
- When it comes to what we sometimes call "work", not make money the primary driver, merely an incidental; and yet, whatever I do needs to feel valued and valuable;
- Look for and respond to opportunities where I can make a real difference to other people; perhaps things that others cannot do just as well or at all;
- In consequence, have the courage and humility to say No to things, even if they are flattering, well-paid and/or interesting; letting go of things that have merely made me feel good;
- To achieve these aspirations, look after my physical, psychological and spiritual well-being;
- Finally, give great thanks every day for what I have: family, friends, worthwhile work to do, time to reflect – and inspiration to write a blog every now and then.

And, of course, in a diverse world, to accept that for some this might read as sanctimonious nonsense. Nevertheless, to use Tim Hicks' words, to continue to stand up and not give up.

Originally published in Kluwer Mediation Blog on 28 September 2020

Holding On or Letting Go?

At this time of year, it is good to reflect, to look back, and also to look forward. This is not always easy as we sense the clutter and complexity of life crowding in on us.

I have had the uneasy experience in the past few weeks of clearing out the Core office, our administrative base for the past several years. With remote working now the norm, not only for delivery but for administration, having a physical office space is, for us, an unnecessary luxury – or more honestly, a glorified and expensive storeroom.

And therein lies the problem. For that storeroom contains gems. Letters from people and clients long forgotten, records of past events, mediations and other fascinating exploits, proposals for unfulfilled projects, ideas which would have changed the world (we thought), articles and adverts (all meticulously logged in hard copy form). From those times when we printed everything out and received letters and enclosures by post, there is so much to read, to reminisce about, to follow up. I've taken to sending photographs (electronically) of long-lost documents to people featured in them – "remember this...", "whatever

happened to...", "a blast from the past...". Some of the recipients respond, others probably shake their heads and click delete.

I found a folder of papers from a project in Africa – that would make a great article or book chapter, I think to myself. I had forgotten how often I had travelled to that great continent on mediation-related work. Records of the wonderful opportunities to support athletes, coaches, funders and administrators in the lead up to the London Olympics and Paralympics in 2012. All the energy put into political dialogue, especially around the independence referendum in Scotland in 2014.

Then, there are all those early strategy papers with detailed action plans. We started so many projects in the early 2000s to promote mediation in different sectors: planning, health, construction, IP, the boardroom, SMEs, the list goes on. And pilot studies, proposed and never taken forward or taken to a certain stage and still undercooked all these years later. Clauses in contracts, ideas for expansion of mediation into deal-making and public/private project management, the list gets even longer. Plus of course, all those interventions and facilitations which made a difference to somebody, somewhere.

Forty bags went off for shredding a week or so ago. A career's worth of endeavour. There are still a few folders to go through — and several boxes of retained papers to sort further, languishing now in my basement at home. That will be a job in itself. When and how to do so? And at what cost to the present with its promise, to looking ahead, to creativity and innovation in the next year?

What is the price for holding on and what value might there be in letting go? More generally, for each of us, what are we clinging on to because we fear the loss in letting go? What would be the impact of releasing ourselves from those things — expectations, unfulfilled ambitions, entitlements, obligations, even our jobs — which confine or restrict us from doing or being what we need to do and want to be going forward? Regularly, as mediators, we ask others these questions. Do we need to ask them of ourselves?

A friend with whom I was discussing all this has leant me a business book by Gino Wickman, entitled *Traction*. Chapter 2 is about "Letting Go of the Vine". The writer tells us that "before you can grow, you'll need to

take a leap of faith." Amongst other tips, he includes simplification, open-mindedness and being vulnerable. Perhaps my challenge, and maybe yours too, is to simplify all that clutter and complexity in life, to be open-minded about the possibilities in the future and to strip away the camouflage and protective armour by being vulnerable in the face of what lies ahead.

There are always options. Usually too many to handle well. As in mediation, we need therefore to identify criteria which we can apply to help us make choices. These are the benchmarks which address our real needs and interests, not simply protecting what has gone before. For me, in simple terms, what criteria will I apply as I endeavour to whittle down still further the contents of those boxes? What are my reasons for holding on to any of it? Nostalgia? Sentiment? Or a real prospect of using the material in a future project, perhaps to the benefit of others who have not been through the same experiences?

More generally, as I consider a new year, what are the benchmarks for assessing how to use my time? There are things I have wanted to do for many years. These are regularly deprioritised as apparently more urgent work comes along, often in the form of the next important mediation.

But there is always a price to be paid. I sense that I need to find the courage to let go of quite a lot of stuff, literal and metaphorical, in order to do the things that really matter to me. What about you?

Originally published in Kluwer Mediation Blog on 28 December 2021

Navigating our Collective Journey:
Where are We on the Boat?

I was privileged to give opening remarks at a meeting of mediators at the International Academy of Mediators, held online during the pandemic. The remarks were a reflection on the times we as mediators are living in. This is an adapted version.

"There is no us and them, only us".

These words were uttered here in Edinburgh in May 2010, almost exactly ten years ago, by our great friend and colleague, Ken Cloke. Ken was addressing the annual meeting of the Church of Scotland, just before it began a debate on same sex relationships among ministers.

"There is no us and them, only us". Never before has this phrase seemed more apt than today. If ever we were in it together, now is the time. I have been struck by the universality of the feelings we recognise, wherever we are. What we are going through is an extraordinary, common human experience.

And yet we are all different too. Our responses are different. How we respond individually is unique in its own way. How each of our countries responds is also different, strikingly so in some cases.

Indeed, it struck me when I woke very early one morning, as I often do these days, that some of us don't need other nations (allegedly) to undermine us with fake news. Some of our own leaders appear to be doing that for us, just fine.

But even those other nations are in this same boat. As Ken Cloke has said, it doesn't matter which end of the boat we are at, if the boat itself is sinking. Never before perhaps has our sheer interdependence been so clear. And the need for radical cooperation. To paraphrase Einstein, the old ways of doing things are unlikely to make us safe again.

So, here is a question for us mediators. Where are we on the boat? Are we going about business as usual, hoping that others are bailing us out? Are we part of the bailing out team? Or are we looking towards those whose hands are on the tiller? Are we making suggestions to those with their hands on the tiller, those who decide where we go?

You may well ask: what locus do we have, as mediators, to make suggestions?

Well, the danger may be that bailing out works to some extent and the boat simply continues in the same direction with the same people in the same situations doing the same things. But where to? Back to hubris, back to business as usual? Is that really where we want to go? Or do we need seriously to consider not only the direction of travel, but how we are getting there?

After all, how we get there is what we mediators are all about. The destination is not so important to us, but how we travel on the journey is critical. So perhaps we do need to have the confidence and the humility to get alongside those with their hands on the tiller.

Recently on the BBC Horizon series there was a magical programme about the Hubble telescope, celebrating its launch from the Kennedy Space Center in Florida, on the space shuttle Discovery, almost exactly 30 years ago. I was there that day, watching at a distance!

What a technological achievement Hubble has turned out to be. On television, the wonderful sights of the universe as seen from Hubble put the coronavirus pandemic into a broader perspective.

It also reminded me of the Voyager spacecraft which apparently may re-enter our solar system 250 million years in the future. Wow, what a journey. Unimaginable really.

At a time like this, we need to remember that we are all on a journey, as individuals and as a species. A remarkable, complex, stimulating, uncertain, humbling, paradoxical journey, full of hope and also of lament. Being as well as doing. Death as well as life. Suffering as well as love.

We mediators are well qualified to help others navigate this unprecedented journey. Not just in our traditional role in conflict resolution, though that remains important, but in what we can contribute more widely to conversations about our collective future.

Originally published in Kluwer Mediation Blog on 28 April 2020

Falling Upward in the Pandemic

When I had an episode of depression several years ago, a friend of mine sent me the book *Falling Upward*, by Richard Rohr, to lift my spirits. That book probably transformed how I view life and helped me to see depression as a gift.

For many, Richard Rohr is the finest theologian writing today. His views are not traditional for they challenge many of the conventions of religiosity. But his insights are remarkable. The premise of *Falling Upward* is that life consists of two parts. The first is about striving, acquiring, ambition, career, status, material things. A world which is black and white, binary, certain. The second stage is recognising how superficial these things are, that the world is uncertain, ambiguous, paradoxical and complex, and that what matters are relationships, interconnectedness, putting others before self. The former approach, Rohr suggests, is unsustainable long term.

Rohr contends that many of us need to go through a life-changing experience to understand and embrace the second stage. This, he says, applies particularly to men of a certain age who may need to experience a sense of brokenness to wake up to the realities of life. We need to fall before moving upward.

It struck me recently that maybe this is what is happening – and indeed may be needed – on a global, societal level. We live collectively as if we must continue to strive, acquire, build careers and empires, gain more and more material wealth and increase our influence. We look at issues as if they were black and white. Leave/remain; yes/no; right/wrong; China and Russia bad/the West good; and so on.

But, in reality, the world is complex and volatile, events are uncertain, paradoxes abound, living as if the planet has unlimited resources is unsustainable. Do we all need to go through a life-changing experience to appreciate this? To be broken in a collective sense? Is this now happening to us as a species, with the pandemic?

As with those who have individual experiences of ill health, the warning signs are often obvious in advance of any breakdown. The pandemic experience is unprecedented. Is it a collective warning of breakdown as well as an example of it? The signals from the planet could not be clearer – breakdown is occurring already.

Perhaps, then, we need to take stock, build relationships, acknowledge our interconnectedness and inescapable reliance on each other at many levels whether we like it or not, put aside our own selfish narrow interests and work hard to find a way to co-exist with those we neither like nor approve of, maintain our courage and humility, and show willingness to take responsibility when we get things wrong. A tall order? Yes, but our futures may depend on it.

Originally published as a Core Blog in February 2021

Some Questions at the Turn of the Year...

This post was developed from a contribution to another event hosted online by the International Academy of Mediators.

There are times when one is not sure what to say or do, especially if one aspires not simply to repeat or anticipate what others might say or do.

What do you say when you don't know what to say? What do you do when you don't know what to do? As a mediator by profession, my response in practice to these questions would probably be to pause, in silence. And do nothing but rather wait to see what happens... In the vacuum of silence, all sorts of things may occur. It takes self-discipline just to hold that space.

And then, perhaps, I might ask a few questions, not always expecting an answer, at least not one expressed as such. As we reflect back on a year like no other for most if not all of us, it seems pertinent to ask ourselves about last year and what it might mean — and indeed what we might take forward from it. So, here are some questions upon which each of us might wish to reflect at the beginning of a new year.

What did we learn last year, about ourselves? Who are we, really, and what really matters to us? What did we learn last year, about our world — and the people in it, and indeed about our own place in it?

Looking back, what do we regret about what we have done or not done — by ourselves, and together with others? And what are we really grateful for? Why?

Who has been kind to us? How kind have we been to others? And to ourselves? How much love have we shared? Really shared?

How will our experience last year change who we are in the coming year? Indeed, how will it change *how* we are, in ourselves and with others? Why might that be important?

Who do we need to speak to soon? Think of someone...What do we really need to say? And who do we really need to listen to? Again, think of someone...What might we hear? What one thing might we do differently this year, as individuals, that will bring real hope to others?

As we reflect on all of this in our professional and personal capacities, and looking ahead, what role as peace-bringers do we each have in today's uncertain world? How will we actually fulfil that role in the new year? What is our unique contribution to our communities?

I was interested to read a report by Carnegie UK Trust reflecting on the role of kindness in the healthcare response to COVID-19, entitled "The Courage to be Kind". Its words speak to us all: *"the ease with which people now speak the language of kindness does little to diminish the tensions and complexities of embedding it in practice. ... the implications of kindness are radical and disruptive."*

The report emphasises the importance of leadership, a concern for others, and the benefits are clear: *"Leadership really matters, and compassionate leadership is associated with high performance, effectiveness, wellbeing and credibility."*

In the best-selling book by the artist Charlie Mackesy, *The Boy, the Mole, the Fox and the Horse*, the horse says: *"Nothing beats kindness, it sits quietly beyond all things."*. At a conference many years ago, I recall asking an older lady what you should do when you don't know what to do. She replied: *"just do the kindest thing"*.

Perhaps these words and our answers to the questions above may offer each of us a guide of sorts as we go forward into a new year, especially in those moments when we don't know what to say or what to do. Happy new year!

Originally published in Kluwer Mediation Blog on 28 December 2020

A version was also published in The Scotsman on 4 January 2021

Reflecting on the Cardinal Virtues and the Liberal Arts

Every now and again something happens to cause me to pause and think – or re-think. Recently, I had that experience at a small ruined castle in the heart of Scotland, near a lovely country town called Edzell.

Edzell Castle, visited by, among others, Mary Queen of Scots and her son, King James VI of Scotland, has a distinctive and well-kept walled garden, which was added to the castle by David, Lord Edzell, in 1604 (just after King James VI became King of England also). It is said that Lord Edzell "clearly intended to stimulate both mind and senses". He certainly achieves the former with a series of carved panels, displayed on the striking walls, which portray the Seven Cardinal Virtues, the Seven Liberal Arts and the Seven Planetary Deities.

I'm not sure I have ever really considered these before now but it was the Virtues and the Arts which got me thinking. I'll leave the planetary gods for another time. To what extent might these ideas from centuries ago still be relevant to our work as mediators?

The Cardinal Virtues are said to be the opposites of the seven deadly sins and include: Faith, Hope, Justice, Charity, Prudence, Fortitude and Temperance.

I suggest that expressing Hope is pretty central to what we do as mediators. For many in dispute, matters have become, or appear to be, hope-less. It is our job surely to underpin what we offer with the hope that those in seemingly intractable disputes can join the millions of others who have nevertheless achieved a satisfactory outcome using mediation. And to persevere with that hope however tough things may seem.

Justice is interesting. One of my favourite writers, the theologian Richard Rohr, writes that "when we think of justice, we ordinarily think of a balance: if the scales tip too much on the side of wrong, justice is needed to set things right... We define justice in terms of what we've done, what we've earned, and what we've merited. Our image of justice is often some form of retribution... When most people say, "We want justice!" they normally mean that bad deeds should be punished or that they want vengeance."

Rohr contrasts that with what many people now call "restorative justice", contrasted with retributive justice. He speaks of the *"total unconditional giving of love"* and of a time when swords would be beaten into ploughshares, when the predatory people in power would lie down in peace with the vulnerable and the poor, when the broken-hearted would be comforted and the poor would receive good news. All very theological, I hear you say. However, do these ideas of "justice" in a restorative sense not conform more closely to what we are seeking to achieve as mediators?

It would be interesting to explore the other Virtues but this is a blog, not an essay! Prudence and Fortitude seem useful to a mediator. As for Temperance...

Returning to the garden walls at Edzell Castle, the Liberal Arts subjects recognised at the time included: Grammar, Rhetoric, Dialectics, Arithmetic, Music, Astronomy and Geometry.

Researching this further, I find that the first three are the "trivium" and the latter four are the "quadrivium". Dialectics has also been referred to as Logic, which I find helpful as the former word has always seemed rather unclear to me. However, I note that dialectics means *"the art of investigating or discussing the truth of opinions"*, or *"discussion and reasoning by dialogue"* and seems to be associated with what we know as the Socratic method. A dialectic is when two apparently conflicting things are true at the same time. Dialectical thinking refers to the *"ability to view issues from multiple perspectives and to arrive at the most economical and reasonable reconciliation of seemingly contradictory information and postures."* As a mediator, you'll see why I was interested... Does this not pretty much sum up what we are trying to help parties in a mediation to achieve?

Rhetoric has always interested me. In a previous career, I was responsible for introducing advocacy skills training at the Scottish Bar. Much of what we focussed on was effective communication or *"creating an event in the minds of the audience in order to persuade"*. Rhetoric is defined as *"the art of creative or persuasive speaking or writing"*, with the rider that it may often appear to lack sincerity or to exploit figures of speech and other techniques. As mediators, do we ever engage in rhetoric – or more likely, observe others doing so (perhaps, for example, in written "position papers" in advance of the mediation day itself)? Can we do more to discuss with others the underlying origins of what we all do and help them to be more thoughtful about how they approach matters?

Again, there isn't space to explore the other Arts except to say this: how often have we mediators found that a basic grasp of Arithmetic has been the key to unlocking a dispute? Just getting the numbers and calculations down on paper or onto the flip chart can give a whole new perspective – and often show that the difference between them is less than parties imagine. And Music? Mediation is surely more akin to the ebb and flow of a good piece of music than to the precision of Geometry, although that precision has its place. In one of the great songs of the 1970s, John Miles sang: *"To live without my music would be impossible to do; In this world of troubles, my music pulls me through."*

Reflecting on the historical background to what we experience day in and day out seems helpful to me as a mediator. Just taking time to consider these Virtues and Arts for this blog has been instructive.

As a coda to this piece, by extraordinary coincidence, just two miles further up the country road from Edzell Castle is the lovely country house called The Burn, which serves as an educational retreat for students and others from around the world. There, many years ago, my mentor, one Michael Westcott, encouraged me to spend two days reflecting on my future career path. That intensive period of creative thinking, in such a beautiful setting, with literally a blank sheet of paper in front of me, set me on my journey from life at the Bar to life as a mediator.

I am forever grateful for these moments of reflection and I am reminded of our individual and collective responsibility to keep re-thinking what we do – and to mentor others to do the same.

Originally published in Kluwer Mediation Blog on 28 July 2021

Argument, Dialogue, Compassion – and Mediation

The former British politician (and leadership contender when the Conservative Party was choosing Boris Johnson), Rory Stewart, is making a mark as an even more independent thinker than he was in the British Parliament.

Recently, he hosted a three-part series on BBC Radio 4 entitled A Long History of Argument. It is worth listening to the series on BBC Sounds if you have access to that app. He traces the history of argument from the Greeks to modern times and notes a marked change from about 2014 when public discourse became much more polarising as the echo chambers of social media began to dominate our communications. The future of democracy *"may depend on rediscovering how to argue well"* he says. The whole series is fascinating and, here, I focus on some of his conclusions and suggestions.

Stewart promotes Citizens Assemblies which can take issues out of the polarised setting of parliaments and enable people to make decisions at local levels of democracy. He favours

a different type of conversation with people talking to each other in small places, encouraged to think more slowly, and to think together rather than separately. He hopes we can regain a sense of empathy, respect and trust, finding ways to persuade without pandering to or manipulating others. Listening, engaging back and forth, navigating the space between, as he describes it. All good mediator territory.

The answer to bad arguments, he says, is not to avoid argument but to argue better, to speak beautifully as he puts it, returning to the ancient Greek art of rhetoric. We should be educated in imagery, metaphor, the poetic analogies that can capture the ambiguity and tension of the world in a way that a simple recitation of mere facts cannot.

He cites the calming and reconciling language of Martin Luther King's I Have A Dream speech and contrasts the *"tasteless falsification, exaggerated rhetoric, false metaphors and lack of careful thought"* of many modern day politicians which intensify resentment and division. He reminds us of the origins of the word: arguere – to make bright or enlighten.

Stewart notes the US philosopher Kenneth Burke's observation that rhetoric can be used in service of insult, bickering, lying and malice but is also crucial to persuasion, cooperation, consensus, compromise, action and ultimately to sympathy, identification and, he concludes at the very end of the series, to love. These are all outcomes which many mediators aspire to help others to achieve.

I was struck by the occasionally seemingly interchangeable use that Stewart makes of the words *argument* and *dialogue*. To my mind, even if used well, argument may still suggest the promotion of a particular point of view. Dialogue, on the other hand, suggests to me a genuine exploration of the issues without a preconceived view of the outcome. It assumes from the start that we don't know it all and need to engage in a *"flow of meaning between or among us"*, as theoretical physicist David Bohm described it. To achieve this is hard work, as we know, and lies at the heart of the work of mediators.

The theologian, Richard Rohr, says this: *"When we can listen and respond in [such a] way, each person*

is treated with the respect and dignity they deserve... Each person feels heard, and misunderstandings are clarified compassionately."

He goes on: *"Unfortunately that is not the way the ego likes to work. Opposition gives us a sense of standing for something, a false sense of independence, power, and control. Compassion and humility don't give us a sense of control or psychic comfort. We have to be willing to let go of our moral high ground and hear the truth that the other person may be speaking, even if it is only ten percent of what they are saying. Compassion and dialogue are essentially vulnerable positions. If we are into control and predictability, we will seldom descend into the vulnerability of undefended listening or the scariness of dialogue."*

As he observes, *"The truth is not well served, [when] neither individual feels secure, respected, or connected. Unfortunately, this has become the state of our public discourse."*

He asks *"Can we take responsibility for the fact that we push people to polarised positions when we do not stand in the compassionate middle?"*

The "compassionate middle". The territory of the mediator. Stewart and Rohr challenge us to keep thinking about how we can use our privileged position to enhance dialogue and compassion in and between large and small groups, especially when forceful arguments are being made by people who are often polarised. We know we add a special kind of value. Our individual and collective futures probably depend on us continuing to offer ourselves in more and more of these difficult situations. If not us, who?

Originally published in Kluwer Mediation Blog on 28 July 2022

Politics and Policy – and Mediation

I am intrigued by the political process and by the need felt by so many for some sort of change in politics and policy-making. The following pieces reflect my own similar views.

Recognising Trauma: Litigation and Politics are Harming Us

I write this in the aftermath of yet another mediation in which the protagonists exhibited symptoms of having been seriously traumatised by the litigation process to which they had been exposed. Depression, suicidal thoughts, anger, loathing, destroyed relationships, large amounts of money spent with no discernible value. And this was a commercial situation, not a family or neighbourhood conflict.

It came to me recently that litigation (in all its forms) is a traumatic event for many people. By that I mean it causes actual trauma, individually and collectively, to many who are caught up in it. My understanding of trauma is superficial, but I now realise that it is more extensive and deep-seated than I had once imagined. Repeatedly exposing people to past events which have caused them pain, revisiting adverse situations, is likely to exacerbate the damage. Is this not just what we do with litigation? By prioritising litigation as a problem-solving mechanism, do we not perpetuate a form of state-sponsored harm, causing untold damage at a societal level?

On the other hand, by giving people control over their present and future circumstances, it seems possible to reduce trauma. That is where mediation fits in of course. It provides, or should provide, what the experts refer to as psychological safety. An opportunity to heal. At an individual and societal level, this seems essential. Perhaps we need to take a much broader view of mediation's value and importance than seeing it merely as an "alternative". And surely this goes wider to embrace how we deal with public dialogue more generally? The adversarial, antagonistic political process we observe these days in many of our democracies seems to legitimise a form of collective trauma, repeatedly reinforcing negative messages, linguistic violence and past misery.

We must do better. Recently, I was privileged to host a conversation between two of the UK's most thoughtful political thinkers, David Melding, former Deputy Presiding Officer of the Welsh Senedd, and Andrew Wilson, chair of Scotland's Growth Commission and former member of the Scottish Parliament.

One committed to a reformed union and one committed to independence for Scotland. The event was characterised by courtesy, mutual respect, dignity and frank exchanges on the issues as both guests looked forward, rather than back, to what could be. Many in the audience commented on how refreshing this was.

By a deft transition, this takes me to the US Presidential election. As the dust settles, perhaps it's time for a re-frame. The world's best attempt so far at democracy has been the subject of much criticism. Arguably, we may have seen the best and worst of democracy in action.

Tens of millions voted freely, in a way that would be impossible in many countries. That the result was so divergent should not be surprising. Voters were presented with what was in effect a binary choice. Like so many decisions taken recently in Western democracies, there is little room for nuance, subtlety, paradox or complexity. It is Yes or No, In or Out, Leave or Remain, Left or Right, Trump or Biden.

With such a limited range of options, and when social media and instant news breeds trivial responses and superficial understanding, it is perhaps inevitable that the arguments have become polarised

and the contests more adversarial – and traumatic. At the crucial stage of decision-making, we have denied richness and, perhaps, got the outcomes we deserve. It has come to be about winners and losers whereas in fact, possibly and ironically, we could all lose in the end. A bit like litigation.

More than that, the binary system provokes our more primitive instincts, including fight or flight and the primeval protective reflex of fear. I sense that fear lies behind many of the unwelcome behaviours we see in politics and organisations more generally. Perhaps having an election during a pandemic, when our collective and individual fears have been triggered more than at any time in the recent past, accentuates this reaction. Fear of loss and the need for self-protection might, paradoxically, again lead to us all losing. A bit like litigation?

This might go further. Reflecting on recent observations by Ken Cloke, we might speculate that, even in a rights-based democracy, if adversarial debate, single truths and win/lose outcomes are commonplace, there is the risk that, when that democracy appears not to be working, some will revert to a more autocratic approach, especially if people are frightened. In that scenario, issues may be simplified, complexity ignored, unrest provoked and fascism may loom. Or anarchy.

While some political strategists and academics will be fully cognisant of these effects of the binary system in the 21st century, most of us are not. Perhaps it's a bit like litigation. Things just go on, habitually, but what damage is being done? We must continue our efforts to expand this discussion and to ask serious questions about how we make important decisions in this era, whether in politics or in dispute resolution.

The task is surely to find ways to move towards a win/win culture, with dialogue as the means to build understanding and consensus in a highly complex, volatile world. We know this is hard work, as we seek to tackle problems together, collaboratively and with humility and mutual respect. But such an approach is more likely to produce sustainable and mutually beneficial outcomes... just as the parties found in the mediation to which I referred at the start of this piece. They were given a place of safety in which they could express and then lay aside their fears. Perhaps even an opportunity to heal. And now they start new chapters, freed from the traumatising effects of the adversarial culture.

Originally published in Kluwer Mediation Blog on 28 November 2020

We and our Politics Must Learn to Deal with Shades of Grey

They say we live in a VUCA world: volatile, uncertain, complex and ambiguous. How true that seems. One tragedy of recent hearings in the Scottish Parliament about the conduct of a former First Minister was how little scope there seemed to be for recognition of nuance, paradox and doubt.

As so often in politics, issues were viewed through the polarising prism of them and us, black and white, binary decision-making. As was once said: *"the contemporary mind has almost no training in how to think paradoxically, being stuck with dualist thought and locked into making seemingly clever distinctions, while devoid of wisdom."* How true that seems.

Experience tells us that there are often two (or indeed many) sides to a story. Shades of grey exist everywhere. That's hard to acknowledge if we crave simplicity, decisiveness and to show that A is right and B is wrong. But two people can see and hear the same events in very different ways. We don't see things as they are but as we are. Perception becomes reality. It's the way we're wired. That reality doesn't make someone a bad person.

Indeed, diversity is what makes us so interesting as a species.

To understand another side, we must challenge our assumptions, put ourselves in the shoes of others. Again, that's hard work, energy-consuming and takes a real effort of will. It requires empathy and imagination.

It's also difficult because of the unconscious biases under which we all labour, leading us to hasty misjudgements and inept conclusions. They may blind us. However, the exponential growth in understanding the way human brains work gives us insight into why we behave as we do – and why others act and react as they do. Let's hope that future inquiries in Scotland and elsewhere will recognise the impact of unconscious bias, both on those who decide and on those who tell their stories.

One such bias arises when we are attracted to explanations that seem to exonerate us, perhaps portraying us as innocent victims, when others question our actions. Under the mask of apparently righteous indignation may lie another reality altogether:

shame and fear of being judged and found wanting. Never under-estimate how far the instinct to save face will drive people. And don't forget confirmation bias, leading to propositions being put which merely reinforce preconceived views and deny the complexity of events.

In future, more insightful inquiries might elicit multiple explanations and deeper understanding on all sides. Perhaps these will not provide political fodder of the ideological sort. But, ironically, by focusing less on the promotion of partisan interests, and more on genuine exploration, greater accountability and responsibility might be achieved, while providing real learning for the future. A challenge for the next Parliament.

For Scotland to succeed as a progressive, compassionate society, we must cultivate more thoughtful ways to address our difficult issues. We need courage and humility to change the conversation, promoting understanding rather than condemnation. This will be hard work, a kind of collective re-wiring. However, there is no other way. In the long run, there is no us and them, only us.

A version of this blog was originally published in The Times on 6 April 2021

Westminster Needs to Brush Up on the Art of Negotiation

It is so frustrating. Whatever the political merits and demerits of saying you will not observe an agreement already reached with another party if it no longer suits you, such a tactic is arguably a really poor negotiation strategy. It is almost bound to produce a sub-optimal outcome for your side.

Such a move appears to come from a school of negotiation that believes that bluster and assertion will cause your counterpart to change its mind. That might work if you have such a powerful position that the other party has no choice but to agree. But if that is not the case, it could be a fatal choice. The danger is that your assumptions are wrong and that you are blinded by your own hyperbole — or weakened by a lack of competence.

Really effective negotiators are skilful and nuanced. They build effective relationships with their counterparts. They know that trust and credibility matter, whatever their differences. The Brexit crisis in the UK over the Internal Market Bill suggests that we may need to educate ourselves, or at least some of our political leaders, in effective negotiation strategies.

It is more than a generation ago that Roger Fisher and William Ury published *Getting to Yes*, probably the most influential work on negotiating, yet so many still follow an approach that is less successful. It was Nelson Mandela who said of the National Party leader in South Africa: "*I never sought to undermine Mr De Klerk for the practical reason that the weaker he was, the weaker the negotiations process.*"

To reach an agreement with your enemy you need, as Abraham Lincoln taught, to work with them, make them your partner. You don't have to like them, agree with their values or be soft. In fact, the more credibly you behave and respectful you are towards the individuals, the more robust you can be on the issues. This is really all pretty basic stuff. Mandela and Lincoln achieved great things in trying circumstances. My goodness, we need their kind of wisdom today.

Perhaps the remedy lies in longer-term thinking. Should we introduce the basics of good negotiation into the school curriculum? It is after all a life skill. We negotiate every day. Let's do it well. More than ever, we need to learn to make the best of limited resources. The best way to do that is to work together to optimise outcomes.

This goes further, of course. It is also about integrity. It is about teaching the next generation that, contrary to what they may observe, it is a good thing to stick by what you promise, to find ways to work with people who may be different and to have principles which you can apply under pressure. If you can do that, history is likely to be on your side.

Originally published in The Times on 22 September 2020

Ditch the Fear Factor in our Healthcare System and Get to Grips with Compassion

Recently I was privileged to give a keynote address to a conference of medical leaders and managers. My title was "Love over Fear in Health Care".

One of the catchphrases in my report into allegations of bullying in NHS Highland in 2019 was: *"Fear cannot be the driver"*. That was prompted by the realisation that many of the human difficulties which occur in the NHS and elsewhere are driven by underlying fear. Fear of being found wanting, of being found out, of being shamed or humiliated, of being blamed or criticised, of not meeting targets and being penalised, of not coping or appearing weak, or of just not meeting expectations, however unrealistic these might be.

Fear like this can be insidious, demoralising, tiring, demotivating, frightening even. It can certainly lead to sub-optimal performance, especially if anxiety becomes widespread. We know that fear can manifest itself in feelings of threat, of anticipated loss (whether of job, earnings, security or status) and that this can result in outbreaks of emotion, sadness and sometimes anger or other aggression directed towards others.

When we feel danger, self-protection – a primitive and essential resource for physical survival but much less useful in social situations – kicks in quickly. This may present symptomatically as anger. The angrier the mask, the more threatened we may actually be feeling. This can so easily overflow into what may be perceived by others as bullying or harassment.

And those perceived as the bullies tragically often feel bullied themselves as the fear rebounds up and down and in and around the system. All of this may become institutionalised, especially if behaviour coming from the top is unhealthy. Dysfunction may fester and spread.

There are so many layers. Underneath the symptoms of anger and aggression, we recognise fear. Strip that away, we are told, and there lies a deeper need, to be loved, appreciated, acknowledged, accepted for who we are and for what we are trying to do.

And yet, so often we look for scapegoats as we seek comfort in our tribes and echo chambers and simply reinforce our assumptions and beliefs, ignoring the often obvious alternative points of view as confirmation bias and wilful blindness kick in. They say we're not divided by our differences but our judgments about each another. Them and us. Villains and victims.

The binary, adversarial world of right and wrong, black and white, in and out, win and lose, discipline and grievance. A transactional world in which we tend to be treated more like widgets than highly complex multi-layered human beings. Where what separates us is given more importance than what we have in common, which is always far greater.

What to do? For me, this is where the love bit comes in. But we're so afraid, embarrassed even, to use that word with its connotations of softness and touchy-feeliness. Perhaps we should call it compassion... or kindness. Whatever word we use, it is not soft at all. It's hard to do kindness and compassion really well. To love is demanding.

To see others, including those who do you wrong, through the lens of compassion, to seek to understand them, takes great courage and self-discipline. To understand that there are, almost invariably, two or more sides to every story: "they" may be just as "right" as you are. Or, as was once said, in retrospect everyone is "wrong". It just depends on your perspective, your standpoint.

To be able to talk openly and candidly, without fear, in safety and security, about what matters to you, is vital. To do so, you don't have to be great buddies with those with whom you work but you do need to respect them and feel respected by them. I would argue that building relationships of respect and trust deserves the same resources and infrastructure as we devote, say, to technological skills.

My experience of countless training courses suggests that building and sustaining relationships of respect and trust can be learned and practised. This is fundamentally a skills issue, honed and refined over time, supported by ongoing professional development.

Originally published in The Scotsman on 5 July 2021

I wrote in similar terms on another occasion, with a few different nuances which I hope justify including this further piece; the reader should feel free to skim:

"Fear cannot be the driver." These words from my 2019 report to the Cabinet Secretary for Health into allegations of bullying in NHS Highland have been quoted on a number of occasions.

I sense that they speak of something deeper in our society with which we must wrestle if we are to address the major challenges facing us now and in years to come. I wonder if fear is endemic in many institutions in our country? Fear of being found at fault, of being blamed, of being placed under intolerable pressure, of losing face, of losing jobs, of being branded a failure?

Where there are hierarchies, fear can be visceral if you are subject to the direction and control of others. But I wonder if fear is also experienced at the very top and all the way through many levels in our organisations? The pressure to perform, to achieve results, to meet targets is probably felt at ministerial level, at chief executive level, at managerial level, as well as at service delivery levels.

Fear may well result in a feeling (whatever the reality) of being bullied. Often those who feel they are being bullied are also perceived by others as bullies. It seems to cut both ways. Our culture of success, of right or wrong, of winners and losers can leave little room for genuine mistakes, human error, experimentation, risk. Instead, it may lead to excessive caution, protection (of self and institutions), unwillingness to innovate, undue deference and reluctance to challenge, parochialism and pettiness.

In economic terms, this is almost bound to result in sub-optimal outcomes. And if someone is in the public eye, these responses may be magnified by the press (exacerbated by instantaneous and relentless social media), political partisanship, short termism and the binary choices with which we are regularly presented: in/ out; leave/remain; yes/no – and so on.

How many of the inquiries and reviews into major public sector expenditure overruns or contractual problems will address the issue of underlying fear which many people caught up in these situations must feel? Indeed, how many of these situations have their origin in a culture of fear? Do such inquiries by virtue of their investigative, often fault-finding, orientation merely perpetuate that fear?

What can we do? Nearly all of us are trying our best, wanting to do well. We must face up to the reality that living in fear won't bring out the best in us. It seems that we need to move away from the blame culture where, every time something does not work as we wish or hope, we must find a scapegoat. We should stop setting unrealistic expectations as if every need can be met in this volatile, uncertain and complex world.

We desperately need authenticity, integrity, courage, and willingness to make sacrifices in the short term for longer term good. Humility rather than hubris. Cooperation rather than confrontation. A willingness to take responsibility and where necessary to admit error, rather than to pass the buck.

Perhaps, above all, we need a good dose of forgiveness and kindness. Too soft, touchy-feely? Actually, no. It's really hard for many of us in this fast-moving, quick to judgment world to pause and engage long enough to replace fear with compassion. But that we must do if we are to thrive and work together for the common good.

Originally published as a Core blog in February 2021

Scottish Independence 'Debate' Requires Empathy and Imagination if it is not to Descend into Verbal Combat

With Scotland's constitutional issue set to take centre stage once again, many will be fearful that division and rancour may follow.

Back in 2014 and in subsequent years, the debate has often generated more heat than light. Arguably, the 2016 Brexit referendum was even more acrimonious.

With the cost-of-living crisis, the troubling scenes from Ukraine, the existential threat posed by climate change and the collective trauma of the pandemic still hanging over many of us, the context in which this latest development arises feels different from 2014. There may be only so much animosity and confrontation that we can take. We need a better way.

This is all about how we handle things. Whatever the substance, namely whether or not Scotland should be an independent country, it surely falls to all of us, particularly those in political leadership arguing for one side or the other, to conduct ourselves with dignity and show respect towards those with whom we may differ.

Indeed, for those who argue for something different from the status quo, demonstrating what sort of country they wish Scotland to be will be enhanced by the manner in which they present arguments. For those who seek to uphold the present arrangements, their conduct will shine a light on why people might choose to support them.

Back in 2014, a diverse group of Scottish citizens, with different views on the constitution, formed a loose coalition called Collaborative Scotland and promoted the Commitment to Respectful Dialogue. Hundreds of people subscribed to it.

Signatories acknowledged that how we engaged with each other may be just as important as any outcome. They affirmed that it was in the interests of a flourishing Scotland that discussions were conducted with civility and dignity. Against that background, they committed to do their best and they encouraged others to do their best to:

- *Show respect and courtesy towards all those who are engaged in these discussions, whatever views they hold;*

- *Acknowledge that there are many differing, deeply held and valid points of view;*

- *Use language carefully and avoid personal or other remarks which might cause unnecessary offence;*

- *Listen carefully to all points of view and seek fully to understand what concerns and motivates those with differing views from our own;*

- *Ask questions for clarification when we may not understand what others are saying or proposing;*

- *Express our own views clearly and honestly with transparency about our motives and our interests;*

- *Respond to questions asked of us with clarity and openness and, whenever we can, with credible information;*

- *Look for common ground and shared interests at all times.*

That commitment nicely sums up what we need now. The binary nature of the constitutional question proposed could mask the complexity of the issue. It's not as easy as black and white, right or wrong, in or out, us and them.

There are layers to this, different sides to the stories, which need to be understood and addressed. Indeed, to call this a debate risks falling into the classic trap of views being expressed in an adversarial way, leading to polarisation and vilification. After all, the word "debate" is apparently derived from the French debatre, meaning to beat down. That cannot be the way to conduct discussions over the next 18 months or more.

We need dialogue, a flow of ideas, recognising the uncertainties, ambiguities and subtleties involved. We must find ways to move beyond the mere stating of positions so that people's underlying concerns, hopes, fears and aspirations are acknowledged, discussed and explored fully.

Just as important is the recognition that whatever happens, we and our politicians need to be able to work together whatever the future holds. Indeed, given the enormity of the other issues which dominate our lives at the moment, we must be able to work together now.

And, if there is eventually a majority, however legally achieved, in favour of change, it seems essential to build and maintain the necessary relationships to enable constructive negotiations to take place in future. The time to be doing that is now, not after a decision is made. All of this should be common ground.

It's easy to say all of this of course. We know how difficult it is to achieve in practice. "It's just politics" was once offered up when I challenged a senior politician on the use of denigrating language towards political opponents.

It may be a certain sort of politics but it creates animosity and undermines attempts to build better relationships. It's a sort of politics that seems unfit for the purpose of discussing the difficult issues that voters are expected to decide on.

We need a more mature, constructive and thoughtful approach all round. Otherwise, for many in the electorate "a plague on all their houses" will continue to be the prevailing sentiment. That's not good for the democratic process, especially when such a profound question is being proposed.

In demonstrations of good leadership, we expect to see self-discipline, humility and the taking of responsibility. Again, this is not easy: blaming others is a natural human reaction and, under the enormous pressure which many will feel, the fight or flight reflex can easily kick in, leading to aggression and defensiveness.

We'll need a good dose of what the Nobel-prize winning psychologist Daniel Kahneman calls "system two" thinking: reasoned, thoughtful, explanatory, overriding the instinctive, protective, combative "system one". We know that this takes conscious effort. It is by definition harder work than defaulting into old habits.

At least we now have much better understanding of these facets of human interaction. In short, doing this a better way will require empathy and imagination on all sides. Can we expect this in the often visceral world of constitutional politics? Many of us believe we are entitled to expect this – and that we must do all we can to encourage and support it.

(The author was co-founder of Collaborative Scotland: www.collaborativescotland.org)

Originally published in The Scotsman on 8 July 2022

This May be the Moment for Mediation in Difficult Political and Judicial Decisions

I am sure that some readers in Scotland watching or reading about the breakdown in relations between our present and former First Ministers will have asked themselves: why don't they try mediation?

This is not as extreme a suggestion as it might appear. Many serious senior level disagreements are dealt with in this way – often with quite unexpected success. Indeed, as Scottish Mediation's recently launched campaign "The Time is Now" reminds us, this is a good moment for Scotland's political leaders to show that mediation offers a constructive way to deal with difficult situations and could make a significant positive impact across our country.

Similar thoughts occurred as I read the Scottish Parliament Rural Economy and Connectivity Committee's report on the construction and procurement of two new ferries for the ferry company Caledonian MacBrayne (CalMac). The Committee outlined difficulties in getting agreement to use mediation to try to resolve the significant contractual dispute. It

expressed the view that "*a process of mediation should have been pursued much earlier and more proactively*". The report narrates the sad breakdown in business relationships and the impact of construction delays on island communities. The potentially massive cost to the public purse is now well known. This is serious stuff for our country and its economy.

Why might it be that, in Scotland (and elsewhere), there remains reluctance and resistance to use mediation in difficult matters? Mediation was mentioned in the context of complaints against the former First Minister. However, some of the evidence suggests that mediation is not well understood. A recently published book by Dr Anna Howard may provide further answers. In *EU Cross-Border Commercial Mediation, Listening to Disputants*, the author has unearthed a number of reasons for the "stubbornly low" uptake of mediation for resolving disputes. We may have been approaching the promotion of mediation in quite the wrong way, she suggests.

Many of us have argued for mediation's use by comparing it with the time, costs, risks, adversarialism and loss of control inherent in an adjudicative process, principally litigation, often in the context of "legally constructed" cases. Howard's main thrust is that framing mediation as an alternative to litigation does not resonate with clients (the actual decision-makers, who rarely use litigation). In approaching mediation narrowly, we have also set it up in apparent competition with litigation and to a lesser extent arbitration. This "oppositional approach" has created awkwardness with courts and justice systems, while some of us appear overly-zealous, relying on "anti-litigation rhetoric".

Ironically, we may have deterred potential users who view disputes more broadly. Far better to promote mediation as a way to help parties to extend negotiations which need some assistance and thus open up a much wider field of opportunity.

However, things are not quite that simple. Howard's research suggests we must acknowledge that mediation asks a lot of disputants. Bringing in a mediator could imply that the parties themselves have not been able to negotiate a solution. It could

thus be perceived as an admission of failure. This perception may be felt by commercial people in whose hands the original negotiation took place (and could also apply to lawyers charged with finding a solution). Users may also fear that any agreement reached in mediation will be viewed as sub-optimal and subjected to criticism by others. Far easier than being a scapegoat is to pass responsibility for the outcome to a third-party decision-maker who can be blamed if the result is unsatisfactory.

Some of this concurs with my own experience, especially in the public sector, where fear of being blamed may lead decision-makers to baulk at mediating or, if they take that step, cause them to back away from making difficult and (to the outsider) necessary choices. That's a perfectly understandable human reaction, albeit potentially costly. Might that explain the CalMac ferry situation?

Might this also apply to civil servants and politicians? Why was mediation not tried in the Brexit negotiations? I recall one civil servant saying, in another context, that they disliked handing over to a third party – perhaps an indication of an underlying fear of appearing to have failed?

All of this points to the need to

continue to articulate clearly the added value which the involvement of a skilled independent mediator can bring to negotiations which need some help, without inferring failure by either the parties or their advisers.

Originally published in The Scotsman on 15 March 2021

(I comment further on Anna Howard's book in a later piece.)

Mediating Inter-Governmental Relations in the UK

I have included the following longer article as the last piece in this section as it exemplifies the potential for mediation to play a role in political matters.

Effective inter-governmental relations among the constituent parts of the United Kingdom are essential in an era of increased devolution of powers, post-Brexit allocation of responsibility and contested narratives about the future of the (uncodified) UK constitution.

Background

One of the rather depressing aspects of the constitutional impasse in the UK is that inter-governmental relations (to which I refer here as IGR) between the UK and Scottish (and indeed the Welsh) Governments have appeared to worsen in recent years. This has been exacerbated in the post-Brexit era with the passing of the UK Government's Internal Market Act, an attempt to address funding and distribution of powers hitherto affected by EU regulation, which has been perceived as a "power grab" by the devolved governments. This has been further exacerbated by perceptions of high-handedness by the present Westminster administration

with its "muscular unionist" approach and difficulties in the implementation of the Northern Ireland Protocol.

There was a time just a few years ago (and I was fortunate to have some minor involvement) when there were active steps to create a more congenial atmosphere for IGR in the UK. But the Joint Ministerial Council and other informal bodies seemed to become less and less effective and to be viewed increasingly as an opportunity for political positions to be staked out. That said, the Covid pandemic and the challenge of climate change (with the hosting in Glasgow of COP26) has necessitated a degree of serious cooperation in these and other areas in the past two years.

IGR Review 2022

However, just recently, a new approach has emerged. Following a review of IGR, new structures have been set out. These, it is said, will *"provide for ambitious and effective working, to support ... COVID recovery,* tackle the climate change crisis and inequalities, and deliver sustainable growth."

The new arrangements are *"built on principles of mutual respect and trust, respecting the reserved powers of the UK Government and Parliament and the devolved competences of the Scottish Government, Welsh Government, Northern Ireland Executive and their legislatures. The new system will provide a positive basis for productive relations, facilitating dialogue where views are aligned and resolution mechanisms where they are not."*

To those of us involved in conflict prevention, management and resolution, this all seems like good stuff and we can note especially the reference to "facilitating dialogue" and "resolution mechanisms" for situations where views are not aligned. The scene is set for language which all mediators will recognise and appreciate. I explore this further in this post.

The Details

More detailed principles for IGR and collaborative working are set out as follows, again with themes which resonate strongly:

"a. Maintaining positive and constructive relations, based on mutual respect for the responsibilities of the governments and their shared role in the governance of the UK;

b. Building and maintaining trust, based on effective communication;

c. Sharing information and respecting confidentiality;

d. Promoting understanding of, and accountability for, their intergovernmental activity;

e. Resolving disputes according to a clear and agreed process."

The review goes on to reaffirm *"our collective commitment to work more effectively together through new machinery"* and that on *"matters of mutual interest, the governments will seek to proceed by consensus, including ensuring the earliest possible resolution of issues."* Among other provisions, intergovernmental machinery should *" b. facilitate effective collaboration and regular engagement in the context of increased interaction between devolved and reserved competence in our new relationship with the EU and other global partners; c. promote dispute avoidance by ensuring there are effective communication and governance structures at all levels, from working-level officials to ministers;"*

Expanding on communication, the following is set out: *"... The governments have committed to effective and timely communication with each other, particularly where one government's work may potentially have some bearing on the responsibilities of another..."*

Under the rubric of dispute resolution and avoidance, all governments *"are committed to promoting collaboration and the avoidance of disagreements... The resolution process ... should be seen as part of a much wider system of active IGR, and as a process of last resort."* Again, this all resonates with mediators and an approach where emphasis is placed on prevention and early management of disputes.

Mediation arrives!

Finally, the breakthrough. One of the functions of a newly established IGR Secretariat is: *"Facilitating the process of dispute resolution. This will include assessing whether the appropriate steps have been followed to resolve a disagreement and decide whether it should be escalated as a dispute through the formal process. Where appropriate, it will appoint a third-party to provide third-party advice or conduct mediation ..., subject to the agreement of all parties to pursue these options"* and later: *"If required, an independent mediator will be appointed, as agreed by the parties to the dispute, on the recommendation of the Secretariat. The timescales for the mediation process will be agreed by the parties."*

This latter provision arises under the heading of "Third-party involvement to resolve dispute", which also provides separately for the "appointment of third-parties to provide advice." There follows some rather confusing text about the need for subject matter expertise (which must be "specific" and/or "extensive") and it will be interesting to see if this is applied to the appointment of a mediator as well as to a third party adviser. Many mediators would argue that, when knowledgeable specialists are engaged by the parties, what you need is a really skilled and experienced mediator, rather than a subject matter expert. The key now is likely to be helping to ensure that there is a really clear understanding of how mediation works and what mediators can add.

Commentary

In the past, reference to an arbitrator or other adjudicative function might have been chosen for dispute resolution. Overall, therefore, this feels like a major step forward, not only in UK IGR, but in recognition of the opportunities offered by mediation to help manage disputes and resolve political differences. This seems both sensible and realistic as it preserves the disputing parties' autonomy to make decisions about whether or not to accept any proposed solution rather than having one imposed.

As we know so well, unless essential, ceding control to a third-party decision-maker, and seeking a definitive determination whether in arbitration or in litigation, can exacerbate and exaggerate differences and divisiveness, as well as being costly and time-consuming, while lacking scope for subtlety and flexibility. Enforcement measures for any decision can become an issue. In political matters, these points seem to have even greater force.

I might observe that the proposed use of mediation could have gone further in this review. In theory, differentiating between disagreements and disputes is a convenient way to manage escalation. It is likely that mediation would be viewed by many as only necessary or appropriate at the "dispute" stage. However, it need not be limited in that way. Mediation can of course be utilised prior to a more formal dispute stage, where it can play a role in reducing risk and achieving better understanding. The IGR Secretariat may in fact play such a role informally.

Had the review gone further, it might have included this wording:

"Notwithstanding the provisions above, the parties may agree at any stage to request the appointment of a mediator to assist them to resolve any difference, disagreement or dispute among them. The IGR Secretariat will facilitate such an appointment."

Interestingly, such a view is consistent with UK Cabinet Office advice on responsible contractual behaviour in the performance and enforcement of contracts, issued in 2020 following the start of the coronavirus pandemic: *"the Government would strongly encourage parties to seek to resolve any emerging contractual issues responsibly – through negotiation, mediation or other alternative or fast-track dispute resolution – before these escalate into formal intractable disputes."*

The Future?

Going even further, of course, there could now be a role for mediation in future discussions about how to address the constitutional issues which seem likely to continue to dominate UK politics in coming years, and the pathway to be followed, including the terms on which any referendums would proceed.

In a stimulating contribution to the early conversations about negotiating Brexit, Horst Eidenmuller wrote this: *"Experience tells us that creating or at least preserving value in extremely complex multi-party negotiations will* be much more likely if mediators guide the parties' negotiations" including negotiations "with a (strong) political or public element." (in *Negotiating Brexit* by Armour and Eidenmuller, 2017, CH Hart, Beck, Nomos, page 117).

The subsequent experience of Brexit negotiations suggests that conventional "positional bargaining" and "value-claiming" approaches to unassisted negotiations continue to result in less than satisfactory outcomes with a tendency towards zero-sum, or lose-lose, results.

Overall, it has been noted (in *Intergovernmental Relations in the UK: Time for a Radical Overhaul?* by Nicola McEwan and others) that *"This major crisis* [the coronavirus pandemic] *has*

thrown into sharp relief the importance of productive working relationships between all levels of government, and has also reminded politicians and publics of some of the profound, shared interests that continue to exist within the UK—and would do so whatever the constitutional arrangements between these territories.

Finding ways to work together more effectively is not just desirable within the current constitutional framework. Even in the event of Scottish independence, or Irish reunification, various kinds of cooperation will still be necessary, by virtue of geography and the continued interdependence of the economies and societies that coexist on these islands."

In UK political discourse, mediation's day may now be coming.

Originally published in Kluwer Mediation Blog on 28 January 2022

A shorter version of this article also appeared in The Scotsman on 14 February 2022

Mediation Practice - and Policy

While the distinction between some of the topics in this section and those in the sections above may appear slight, the following are, I think, more closely linked to actual mediation practice.

I'll See You on the Dark Side of the Moon: Reflecting on Rapport, Trauma and Resonance in Mediation

"It's hard to beat Dark Side of the Moon" he said. *"What a piece of music."* I agreed: *"Did you ever see Pink Floyd play Dark Side live? I recall being at Earls Court in 1994."* *"I was there too!"* he exclaimed. For a moment or two, we reflected on the album's seemingly relevant song titles, like "Us and Them".

It was about 4.15pm on the mediation day. We had gathered the key players and their lawyers together in a plenary session to take stock of progress. One of the lawyers had a collection of vinyl LPs in view on the Zoom screen. This had stimulated an earlier conversation about music, in that lawyer's private room, with his client. As we gathered now for this later session, I chose to use that earlier conversation as a way to start the meeting, by commenting to the other side's principal decision-maker, a business turnaround expert, that he and I had not discussed his musical tastes. He had turned his camera round to show his collection of albums, leading to the Pink Floyd comment – and a completely spontaneous conversation then arose between the clients about their respective musical tastes.

On another occasion, while meeting a party for the first time in a preparatory meeting to test out comfort with using Zoom, I asked her partner, who was present to provide support, what he was doing to fill in time during lockdown. *"Making a model of a Lancaster bomber,"* he told me. *"Fancy that"* I was able to reply, *"One of my pandemic jobs has been to go through some old boxes containing papers from my father. Just the other day, I was reading his navigator's log from his time flying on Lancasters in the Second World War."* Not only that but when we next met on the mediation day, I was able to show him my own Lancaster model from 1965!

Mere passing moments you may think. Perhaps not. With mediation now taking place online during the pandemic, and every prospect that this will continue after the worst of the pandemic is over, we don't have the same opportunities to build and sustain rapport with people as we might do naturally when in the same physical space. We can't shake hands for example, a human ritual with powerful effects and ancient origins (see the recently published book, *The Handshake*, by Ella Al-Shamahi). We need therefore to take new opportunities to generate rapport as they arise. Not only that but to look for and even create such opportunities. The two exchanges described here (adapted slightly for this post) completely changed the tone of an important plenary meeting in the first case and built confidence and provided reassurance in the second.

I have come to think that this goes further. In a previous piece, I discussed the traumatic effect that engaging in litigation must have for many people, the harm it must cause. Participating in mediation can be traumatic too when it arises in the context, as it so often does, of an ongoing dispute or conflict between people who hold different views and have experienced the entrenching of positions. For those involved, however different we hold out mediation to be, there is often anxiety attached. Our job is to reduce that as much as possible and engage people in constructive activity.

We know that conflict can promote separateness, self-protection, a silo-mentality. In a recent conference on trauma, I was interested to learn that this response resides in the left hemisphere of the brain. It affects how we see the world. Under pressure, we know that our fight, flight or freeze response is engaged. Apparently, when we live in fear, the left hemisphere of the brain is dominant. The majority of us apparently view life through the left hemisphere with no real sense of who we are. The way of the world at present, placing many of us under chronic stress and hyper vigilance, pulls us in that direction and away from the warmth of relationships. We are told that the pandemic has robbed many of us of our social and cellular systems of protection. The absence of close physical proximity induces a higher stress response. The neural impact of chronic stress can cause changes in the brain structure. The right hemisphere of the brain, that part which builds connections, relationships and warmth, and slows us down, is damaged by trauma.

In our conference, we learned about the autonomic, parasympathetic and sympathetic nervous system, neuroception and its connection to perception. We explored the importance of the ventral vagus as our safety system and the dangers of what is referred to as the dorsal state. The former enables connection, resourcefulness, option generation, hope and compassion. The latter results in numbness, hopelessness and loss. And so on. For me, it was both a revelation and strangely familiar, as if I had alighted on a parallel explanation of what I have learned as a mediator.

A question for the conference was how to engage the right hemisphere, to reduce the damage caused by chronic stress. We learned about resonance, recognising that what the human brain craves more than anything else is to be understood, to be accompanied and not alone. We were told that words are crucial. Language, originally a grooming or connecting process for apes, became used over time in a more left hemisphere, technical, mechanistic way (I note the proximity of this thinking with the fascinating insights in Joseph Henrich's recent book *The Weirdest People in the World: How the West Became Psychologically Peculiar and Particularly Prosperous*).

Often, our language causes loss of connection. If it promotes left hemisphere activity, we see others as instruments to achieve our goals.

On the other hand, we can change everything, including our relationships with others and their stories, by what we say, by the way we talk. This takes us back of course to the non-violent communication about which so many of us learned half a generation ago from Marshall Rosenberg.

As I write this, I am reminded of another recent book which addresses how we can deal with mental health issues, in ways which resonate for me as a mediator: *Chatter: The Voice in Our Head, Why it Matters and How to Harness It* by Ethan Kross. "*Changing the conversations we have with ourselves (and with others) has the potential to change our (their) lives.*" (Bracketed words added by me). That book would merit a post on its own.

To the importance of language, we add the safety cues discovered in the upper third of the face, including the eyes; the impact of what we hear; and the music and rhythm of the voice and tone, as another cue for danger or safety.

All of this should of course be meat and drink to the mediator. Think about its application in what we do — and the verification this provides for what we have learned, often by instinct. Think about this in the context of building rapport on Zoom, of finding ways to engage the right hemisphere, of reducing the traumatic impact of conflict, of resonance and the brain's need for understanding and accompaniment, of the impact of words we use at critical moments, of the way our voices can help to change the story.

And Dark Side of the Moon? The Lancaster bomber? I venture to suggest: much more important than we might think.

Originally published in the Kluwer Mediation Blog on 28 March 2021

Mediations, using Zoom – a Revelation?

Ten weeks ago, I had barely heard of Zoom. At that time, I was fairly sceptical about online mediation in the kind of cases I do. It could never substitute for face-to-face meetings with their intimacy and candour. Or so I thought.

I have recently undertaken a number of mediations using Zoom. It is, frankly, a revelation. Indeed, in some respects for me as a mediator, this format is proving to be more effective than the traditional way.

Why might that be? Well, our preparation is different. In advance of the "mediation day", I have met with the parties (the principals), and had one or more detailed meetings with the lawyers to discuss preparation, further inquiries and the issues and to focus on key points. All of these meetings have involved using Zoom albeit, in one case, only after a telephone conversation with the client and his lawyer and two experimental further calls to explore and then demonstrate Zoom. Initial reluctance changed to acceptance.

In a number of cases, in the initial meetings, I have shown the parties and their lawyers how the breakout rooms work, moving them back and fore between different locations in different permutations. That has built real confidence. All documents come separately and electronically. There is less formality about documentation, enabling people to augment and modify as the discussions progress. The (modified for this format) agreement to mediate is signed electronically in advance.

As a result, in advance of the "mediation day", I feel I have been able to focus better not only on the substantive issues but on personal dynamics and sensitivities. Of all my learning, though, it's the intimacy of the meetings on the day which impresses me, whether listening to a party explaining his or her story, or discussing privately with the lawyers as candidly as I have ever done, their negotiating strategy and how I can help them. Sometimes, we have done this in the lawyer's separate room, giving their client another room, indeed with permission to go off and do other things until their lawyer texts them with a request to return.

Sometimes I have spoken to the parties on their own just to reassure and help them to manage the day. Sometimes the lawyers all gather in the "lawyers' room" to take stock. While many of the usual negotiation dynamics are present, I am finding that there is often greater candour and more respect shown for differing views. And a willingness to assess the effect of how we speak and act online. It is as if this electronic distancing enables a different kind of intimacy or openness.

I feel I have been able to be as frank and as considered as I would always hope to be. I am less hassled than I sometimes feel moving between rooms. We laugh about sharing lunch and refreshments. Dress code seems to vary but is mostly more relaxed and variation is not an issue. I feel more in control and of course, in a way, I am.

The real point, however, is that this is not a "Zoom mediation" but a mediation using a number of media, including an online visual and audio tool which is called Zoom. The platform is a servant to the process, not the other way round.

Another, separate, thought has occurred to me as we ponder the delay in court cases. I have been struck by the effect on parties of long-running court cases. I have had some situations recently where the human cost of delay and the accumulation of physical and mental damage, and of monetary damages as a result, is really significant. By being stuck in the litigation process, people who are already suffering become even less able to get back to work and even more psychologically damaged. Medical and employment reports will often say that, until a case is resolved, the claimant will not be able to move on. And yet they wait for months or years... This is, arguably, a scandal. I know this is an obvious point but, if ever there was an argument for trying something different as a speedy alternative, now is surely the time.

And, as I have argued in another article, online mediation could make a substantial contribution to lowering the carbon footprint of dispute resolution.

Originally published in Kluwer Mediation Blog on 29 May 2020

Abraham Lincoln Sought Compromise. So Should We.

"Discourage litigation. Persuade your neighbours to compromise whenever you can. Point out to them how the nominal winner is often a real loser, in fees, expenses, and waste of time. As a peacemaker the lawyer has a superior opportunity of being a good man. There will still be business enough." These are the words of Abraham Lincoln over 150 years ago.

It is said that Lincoln was a skilled lawyer and a formidable opponent in the court room. And yet he was keenly aware of the limitations, unpredictability and risks of pursuing litigation, even if successful. Lincoln encouraged negotiation wherever possible. He was able to set aside his own ego and emotions and put his clients' interests first.

Much more recently, in 1983, the then Chief Justice of the United States, Warren Burger, addressed the American Bar Association. He pointed out that "The entire legal profession – lawyers, judges, law teachers – has become so mesmerised with the stimulation of the courtroom conflict that we tend to forget that we ought to be healers of conflicts." He asked: *"Should lawyers not be healers?*

Healers, not warriors? Healers, not procurers? Healers, not hired guns?"

Mahatma Gandhi observed: *"I understood that the true function of a lawyer was to unite parties riven asunder."* In other words, Gandhi recognised that many clients want peace and harmony in their lives and lawyers can facilitate that. The real goal should be maintaining dignity on both sides, whether the parties are corporations or married couples. How well do lawyers achieve that?

Perhaps lawyers have been perceived as generally cautious, risk averse and concerned with maintaining the status quo. These characteristics may well be a function of legal education which has placed emphasis on linear thinking, logical causation and rational analysis, a kind of mechanistic Newtonian worldview, with attention paid to minutiae. That may have been appropriate in an apparently simpler world. However, to extend the scientific analogy, the volatile complexity which underpins quantum physics tells us that things are much less certain and more ambiguous than we have traditionally thought.

Never has this been more true than today. When it appears that the courts may be unable to handle thousands of cases in the months and even years ahead, the words of Lincoln, Burger and Gandhi seem particularly apposite. Big picture thinking is essential. Lawyers as agents of change may feel uncomfortable and unfamiliar. But there is no choice. Adaptation to new ways of doing things is no longer optional. Changes which may have taken years are now happening in weeks.

We'll want to find more creative ways to help clients resolve disputes than relying on the justice system, even as a backdrop in which the "shadow of the court" provides some sort of incentive to settle. Working with clients as early as possible to negotiate a sensible outcome will call on the skills of lawyers in every area of practice. The current situation presents a real opportunity to encourage the kind of step change in addressing disputes which will fit well with the ambitions of Scotland's National Performance Framework – and reflect the aspirations of Lincoln and others. The use of online technology, collaborative problem-solving, mediation and other effective ways to encourage cooperative solutions is likely to be central.

I have been impressed at how effective an online platform such as Zoom can be. Until recently, I would have argued that online mediation was an inadequate substitute in the kind of cases I undertake where face-to-face meetings seem so important. However, while not pretending that the atmosphere is the same, my reservations about establishing relationships using video have fallen away to a considerable extent. I am surprised and encouraged by what can be achieved. At a time when neither face-to-face mediation nor most court trials are likely to occur for the foreseeable future, this becomes an acceptable alternative which also minimises travel and other costs associated with using physical space. That should not be overlooked as we seek to find ways to reduce the carbon footprint of dispute resolution.

We are entering a New Era. Change is not optional. Our ability to embrace it is likely to define our individual and collective futures. There will still be business enough.

Originally published in The Scotsman on 25 May 2020.

The Costs of Litigating

The Times newspaper reported on a bitter boundary dispute between two pensioners, each in their eighties, over a strip of land less than a metre wide. Apparently, the legal battle has cost them £500,000, contributed to the death of a spouse and caused stress-related illness. The parties have been engaged in a seven-year dispute at Perth Sheriff Court. Now the Sheriff is urging them to drop the case, saying that it is difficult to identify the benefit in continuing to litigate when judged against the effort and expense involved.

It is hard to believe that this has gone on for so long and at such cost. Unfortunately, these situations occur and people end up in prolonged disputes in courts where the cost, time and stress often exceeds the benefits even to those who get a decision in their favour. As Abraham Lincoln once said: *"Discourage litigation. Persuade your neighbours to compromise whenever you can. Point out to them how the nominal winner is often a real loser – in fees, expenses, and waste of time."* How apt.

Of course, achieving compromise also requires those giving advice to do all they can to help their clients to find a consensual solution. When gender equality in the legal profession was not as well established as it may now be, Lincoln went on to say: *"As a peacemaker the lawyer has a superior opportunity of being a good man. There will still be business enough."* In the reported case, it is possible that the lawyers, who would know from experience how traumatising litigation can be for those involved, did all they could to try and persuade the neighbours to find a compromise. If so, one would then look to the court to take the initiative at an early stage in proceedings to avoid the seven years of conflict these people have gone through. Many lawyers and courts would do just that.

Recently, an expert group (of which I was co-chair), established by Scottish Mediation and supported by the Scottish Government, made a number of recommendations for greater and earlier use of mediation in Scotland. It recognised that, in Scotland, we may have fallen behind some other jurisdictions in making mediation widely available across all sectors, not merely as an alternative to going to court but as a way to help disputing parties find an agreed solution when they get stuck in their negotiations.

The Group's report, *Bringing Mediation into the Mainstream*, acknowledged that, with the help of a mediator, relationships can be maintained and restored, much time and cost saved, more creative outcomes arrived at and considerable stress and anxiety avoided. Experience shows that this applies as much to commercial and professional situations as it does to families and neighbours.

In modern Scotland, what happened in Perth Sheriff Court should be a thing of the past. It falls to the Government, courts, policy-makers, legal advisers and the rest of us to encourage our friends, colleagues and neighbours to use mediation more. We'll all benefit.

Originally published as a Core blog in January 2021; a version of this appeared in Scottish Legal News on 3 February 2021.

Time to Regain Momentum on the Benefits of Mediation

I have written many times about the benefits of mediation. I have been aware of the dangers of overkill, special pleading ("he would say that wouldn't he") or being a prophet without honour in his own land.

However, recent developments south of the border in England prompt me to return to the mediation theme. Momentum is gathering elsewhere and, after a flourish a couple of years ago, I worry that Scotland might fall behind. This is important as those who have disputes to resolve may go where the system appears more flexible and progressive.

Mediation has often been used interchangeably and misleadingly with the term "alternative dispute resolution" (ADR). In April, Sir Geoffrey Vos, Master of the Rolls and head of civil justice in England and Wales, said that he disliked the label "alternative" for non-court dispute resolution and he wanted the process moved into the mainstream. He observed: *"ADR should no longer be viewed as alternative, but as an integral part of the dispute resolution process; that process should focus on resolution rather than dispute."*

More recently, a report from the Civil Justice Council (CJC) in England and Wales, led by Lady Justice Asplin, described ADR as a collective term for all dispute resolution methods, of which mediation is probably the most significant, where third parties assist people to explore resolution of a claim. Recognising existing compulsory initiatives, but also marking a departure from a landmark case seventeen years ago, the report concluded that requiring parties to attempt ADR at a certain stage or stages and/or permitting the court to make an order to that effect would be both lawful and "potentially an extremely positive development".

With successful outcomes being achieved in the large majority of mediated cases, this makes sense, especially when the costs of litigating are often disproportionate to the sums in dispute in the case. As a mediator, I have lost count of the number of cases where the settlement amount agreed in mediation is less than the total legal costs to date and where costs become the major sticking point.

The report recognised that *"more work is necessary in order to determine the types of claim and the situations in which compulsory ADR would be appropriate and most effective for all concerned."* There is no one-size-fits-all approach. A number of questions arise: What form of ADR is appropriate for different types of case and at what stage? Are some cases better suited than others? Might ADR be disproportionate in terms of time and cost having regard to the amounts at stake?

Remember that no one is saying that parties to a dispute can be compelled to come to an agreement in mediation. Only that they may be required to try it. As the CJC report confirms, the common feature of the various ADR techniques is that parties at all times retain the ability to refuse to settle and return to the court if they wish to do so.

As one observer commented: *"Making ADR mandatory does not guarantee that cases settle, but you do create more opportunities for the rational assessment of litigation risk and to agree on remedies that the courts cannot provide."*

The UK Government's recent consultation on 'Reforming Competition and Consumer Policy' includes proposals to increase the uptake of ADR as a way to support consumers. In particular, the Government is seeking views on whether to make business participation in ADR mandatory in the motor vehicles sector and the home improvements market.

Following the CJC report, the UK Ministry of Justice has launched a call for evidence on the best ways to settle family, business and other civil disputes without resorting to litigation, with this message:

"For far too long the so-called "alternative" approaches to court have been seen as an add-on or diversion for people seeking to resolve a dispute... We want to support people to get the most effective resolution without devoting more resources than necessary – financial, intellectual and emotional – to resolve their dispute."

This is not just about compulsory ADR. It is also about how to ensure that all cases are resolved quickly, cost effectively and fairly, especially post-pandemic. The key therefore seems to be engaging with the detail rather than the principle. Have we reached this stage in Scotland? If not, now is a good time to regain momentum.

Originally published in The Scotsman on 23 August 2021

Legal Action can be Costly, but There are Alternatives

"Isn't it incredible where you end up in a situation where the small guy cannot take on the big guy because they cannot afford the legal action?" "That's an incredible situation – no justice can be served unless you can afford it." These are words of Edinburgh South MP Ian Murray, referring to concerns about Partick Thistle Football Club's inability to challenge the Scottish Professional Football League's decision to relegate the club this season. As it happened, Thistle later received financial support to enable it to join Heart of Midlothian Football Club in that club's petition to the Court of Session.

More recently it was reported that the clubs responding to the case, Dundee United, Raith Rovers and Cove Rangers, have set up a crowd funding campaign to help finance their legal bills in the subsequent arbitration. The predicted costs are reported to be in six figures.

In a recent article in the New Statesman, the economist Paul Collier expressed the view that *"nobody is cheering the two professions that Britain rewards most generously: the City bankers and lawyers to which our clever youth have gravitated. And nor should we: they are two professions liable to do the most damage to our economy during crisis."*

This is strong stuff. And it does not do the legal system or profession good to be the subject of such commentary which, it is appropriate to recognise, probably goes right back to Charles Dickens and the fictional court case of Jarndyce and Jarndyce in the novel Bleak House where *"the legion of bills in the suit have been transformed into mere bills of mortality"*. And those in Scotland might argue that the New Statesman article is more pertinent to high profile causes in the courts and scandals in financial institutions south of the border. But it all sticks of course.

I do not seek to argue that legal costs are not or will not be properly incurred. They are a feature of the way the system has developed as those within it seek to provide high quality services. Indeed, along with many others, I have been a beneficiary.

However, might the time have come to consider what can be done to address these concerns? Could the courts and the profession be clearer in explaining to the general public and potential court users why costs can be so high and therefore why some potential litigants must be excluded or compelled to resort to other sources of funding?

Indeed, is it preferable and equitable for some to be compelled to seek out alternative ways to fund such cases? (I note an article just a few weeks ago about commercial litigation funding, which can provide reassurance for some clients.) Is this a valid approach to accessing justice? Could we make more use of pro bono or lower cost initiatives to ensure greater access? What else could be done?

While there will always be a relatively small number of cases in which legal rights need to be adjudicated upon, as readers might expect I would also express the hope that more and more disputes would be negotiated to a satisfactory conclusion without the need to go to court at all, whether by using the services of mediators or (preferably) because lawyers and other advisers have the skills to do so themselves. The majority of disputes do resolve in this way and many Scottish lawyers are adept at this.

With the Covid-19 pandemic, matters have become more acute. Courts and lawyers around the world are encouraging alternative options to help deal with the number of cases which are likely to be caught in a backlog.

Indeed, in May, the UK Cabinet Office issued an interesting and forward-looking guidance note on *"responsible contractual behaviour in the performance and enforcement of contracts impacted by the Covid-19 emergency"*. The note strongly encouraged those with disputes to *"to seek to resolve any emerging contractual issues responsibly – through negotiation, mediation or other alternative or fast-track dispute resolution – before these escalate into formal intractable disputes"*.

Negotiation, mediation, or other alternative or fast-track solutions – for many potential and actual disputes, that must surely be the way ahead.

Originally published in The Scotsman on 20th July 2020.

Mediation and Juicing – Parallel Worlds?

One of the positive aspects of the enforced changes brought about by lockdown is that it enables – or compels – us to try new things.

In some ways, amidst all the hardships, what a time this is. A time of innovation, surprises, deep reflection and some profound challenges.

For me, there was another surprising novelty which only arose because of the strange times in which we live. It created an unexpected juxtaposition of ideas as we reflect on attitudes towards mediation. Bear with me while this unfolds.

My wife and I felt we needed a break of some sort. We could not travel. However, for some time I have been following an interesting enterprise offering "juicing" detox retreats. Yes, juicing. *The Body Tool Kit* is a project run by Katrina Mather, attracting people from all over Europe and elsewhere to scenic, isolated spots in Scotland for a week of rest and recuperation, being nourished only on fruit and vegetable juice (and some soup in the evening). Reflecting the spirit of the age, Katrina has now taken these retreats online.

For six days, we met on Zoom four times a day with our fifteen fellow juicers, each consuming our pint of remarkable concoctions, all mixed at home (our garage was full of fruit and veg!). We learned not only about the restorative benefits of juicing (and giving your digestive system a real break) but about the impact of Big Pharma and Big Food on our diet and medication – just watch Jason Vale's Super Juice Me and Joe Cross's Fat, Sick and Nearly Dead for inspiration.

We learned about toxicity, stress, inflammation, the gut/brain connection, the adverse impacts of antibiotics, earthing, magnesium, hydrotherapy, 16-18 hour fasting and so on. All delivered warmly, knowledgeably and without hyperbole. Fascinating. Incidentally, I lost nearly half a stone and my excess midrift. I've been more or less off caffeine since. But all that is incidental to the learning and longer-term healing benefits. Juicing permits the body to heal itself. It recognises, or mediates, the relationship between the body and diet. It detoxifies.

With the hint at the end of that last paragraph, what has this got to do with mediation I hear you ask? Well, it was midway through the week when the penny dropped. I'd done a bit of research online and, to be honest, was rather sceptical when I read the scientific studies and discovered the apparent absence of evidence based and fully researched support for the benefits of juicing. In fact, on day one, I almost contemplated quitting when I had finished my Google searching.

But then someone (the GP in our group, I think) mentioned that doctors receive very little training at medical school in nutrition and its benefits and can tend simply to prescribe medication for our ailments, which often deals with symptoms rather than underlying causes. This can become a habit, the way things are done. Sometimes the economic models for medical services are dependent on pharmaceutical companies and their funding. Juicing is viewed as AMT: "Alternative Medical Treatment". Very much an afterthought and rather dismissed. And yet the anecdotal evidence of its value is significant. For many people with a medical problem, it may offer a real long-term remedy. It could be argued, in many cases, that conventional medicine (and medication) should perhaps be the last resort, the final "alternative". For it can be toxic to the body.

The parallel with mediation soon became striking. Training in negotiation and mediation is rather limited in most law and business schools. It can seem cursory, a bit of an afterthought. Resistance among practitioners and policy-makers is regularly attributed to lack of an evidence base for success, although all those of us with experience know, anecdotally, of mediation's benefits in most (all?) cases. It offers real long-term remedies in many situations. Mediation can help parties to heal themselves. It mediates the relationship between people and their problems in difficult situations. It detoxifies.

However, the legal system can appear to be set up to prescribe litigation as a regular antidote to disputes – or at least to tend to favour adversarial, polarising negotiation strategies. Often only the symptoms are being addressed, rather than the underlying causes. This can become a habit, the way things are done. Sometimes there is an economic interest in doing so. We know that mediation, as "Alternative Dispute Resolution", is often not the first choice, can even be an afterthought and rather dismissed. Yet, in many cases, it could be much more sensible to view litigation (or antagonistic negotiation) as the true last resort, the final "alternative". For litigation can be toxic to parties' commercial, professional and personal relationships.

An important caveat: many doctors and many lawyers subscribe to and offer holistic advice. And of course there are times when conventional medication is essential, a life saver, just as on occasion a robust approach is needed in disputes. As ever, it is a question of considering where the balance lies.

Mediation and juicing: parallel worlds, parallel experiences, much to contemplate. It is only by experimenting with new things, innovating and being prepared to be imaginative, that progress can be made. In this new era, we will need innovation and imagination, and to try new things, even if that means for some of us accepting the lot of the pioneer, as a prophet without honour in her or his own land.

Originally published in Kluwer Mediation Blog on 28 June 2020

Changing the Frame: Some Challenging Issues for Promoting Mediation

Dr Anna Howard's first book, *EU Cross-Border Commercial Mediation: Listening to Disputants – Changing the Frame; Framing the Changes* (published by Kluwer), is an important contribution to the literature about the practice and promotion of mediation. It deserves a wide readership among academics and practitioners alike.

While focused on commercial mediation in the context of cross-border disputes in the EU, the book poses a number of fundamental questions for all those who have wondered about the "stubbornly low" uptake of mediation as a process for resolving disputes. Anna Howard's meticulous research, both deep and broad, invites us to consider new angles to this perennial conundrum, particularly from the perspective of those who would actually choose to use mediation.

A Different Reference Point for Mediation?

For me, this book provided several light bulb moments. I suspect that, for many of us, it may suggest that we may have been approaching the promotion of mediation in quite the wrong way. The main thrust is that the EU, in its attempts to promote its mediation Directive, has framed mediation as an alternative to litigation. However, having carried out research among those who are actually responsible for choosing whether or not to use mediation as a means to help resolve cross border commercial disputes, namely in-house legal advisers in mainly large companies, the author has discovered that this framing does not resonate with them.

In fact, for these decision-makers, the reference point should be negotiation, not litigation. They view mediation as an extension of the negotiation process in which they all engage much more than any other dispute resolution method. Litigation is after all relatively rarely used in most commercial (or indeed any) dispute resolution. Negotiation is the standard process for most people. For those of us who have always viewed mediation as a way to help parties whose negotiations are stuck, this seems an obvious point. But, although we may see it that way, most of us have argued for mediation's use by comparing it with the time, costs, risks, adversarialism and loss of control inherent in an adjudicative process. And, like the EU, we've called for proposals which address these. This may suit those who wish to reduce civil justice budgets but it may fundamentally miss the point about the value which mediation adds, in and of itself.

In doing so, we have set mediation up in competition with litigation and to a lesser extent arbitration and other adjudicative procedures. This "oppositional approach" has created awkwardness with courts and justice systems. It has made some of us seem zealous or evangelical, relying on "anti-litigation rhetoric". And, as this book reveals, it does not resonate with users. While the author is careful to confine her conclusions to her field of study, I believe that the reasons she uncovers are likely to apply more widely. That is important because, while promoting mediation more explicitly as an assistance to parties with their negotiations opens up a much wider field of opportunity (whatever happened to "deal mediation"?), it also requires us to wrestle with the reasons expressed by the users for not wishing to call in a mediator to assist with negotiations.

Fear of Failure?

It is in this discussion that I feel this book is really valuable. To invite a mediator to help is to admit that the parties themselves have not been able to negotiate a solution. It is thus perceived as an admission of failure. Often this perception is felt by the commercial people in whose hands the negotiation has taken place, especially if the suggestion for mediation comes from those charged with finding an alternative way to resolve the dispute. Not only that but users fear that any agreement reached in mediation will be viewed as sub-optimal and subjected to criticism by others. Far better to abdicate responsibility for the outcome to a third-party decision-maker who can be blamed if the result is unsatisfactory.

I have to confess that these points concur with my own experience, especially in the public sector, where fear of being blamed often leads decision-makers to baulk at mediating at all or, if they take that step at least, causes them to back away from making brave and (to the outsider) necessary choices. The ultimate cost to the taxpayer is often greater but it is easier for the court to be held responsible for ordering a course of action. It's a perfectly understandable human reaction.

(The thought has occurred to me that this fear of admitting failure may also apply to civil servants and politicians. Why, many of us have asked, was mediation not tried in the Brexit negotiations? I recall one civil servant saying to me, in another context, that they did not wish to hand over to a third party – perhaps this was an indication of an underlying fear of losing control or appearing to have failed.)

As the book suggests, all of this points to the need to change the frame and articulate clearly the added value which the involvement of a skilled outside mediator can bring to unassisted negotiations which become stuck, without inferring failure by the parties. It also points to the need to address wider issues of responsibility and accountability in our commercial and public sector cultures. Fear, blame, binary choices and scapegoating are all too familiar especially when resources are limited and zero-sum choices seem all that is available. Against that backdrop, the book is right to suggest that we need to acknowledge that mediation asks a lot of many disputants.

Enforcing Mediation Agreements – the wrong approach?

Another significant finding addressed in this book is how unimportant enforceability of mediation agreements is for the interviewees. They go further: mediation agreements are freely entered into contracts like any others which spring from commercial negotiations. Their comments suggest that there is no rational basis for according the former preferential treatment over the latter. Indeed, it is arguable that to do so is unsound in theory. Speaking for myself, I have always considered the initiative which led to the Singapore Convention on enforceability of mediation agreements to be misconceived and to confuse a contract, reached by consensus with the help of a mediator, with a third-party imposed court order or arbitration award. This book offers the user affirmation of that very point, "a solution in search of a problem" as one interviewee put it.

I do wonder if the prevalence of erstwhile litigation lawyers in mediation policy-making and practice has led us to an unfortunate place, both in the narrow sense of the Singapore Convention and more generally in the way mediation has been presented to the outside world? Of course, it has rather suited us to present mediation in a particular way as it plays to our knowledge and skills but have we done it a great injustice, even come close to throwing the baby out with the bathwater? As this book points out, mediation is often grouped with litigation and arbitration as a third party process, often in the context of "legally constructed" cases. If we think about it, this is a fundamental error of categorisation and almost bound to deter many potential users who view disputes much more broadly.

Challenging Our Views?

Do you find yourself resisting these observations and questions? For those of us who have staked a lot in recent years on a particular approach to promoting mediation, that would be understandable. But the point of, and made in, this book is that we need to step back, take stock, avoid a merely reflexive response and be deliberate and curious in our approach. One of its charms is its regular recourse to more philosophical sources for inspiration. Drawing extensively on the writing of John Paul Lederach, Anna Howard reminds us that the obvious answer may be right in front of us, but that we are blind to it. We need to challenge our predetermined solutions and confirmation biases – and be prepared to change our framing.

Indeed, referring also to the excellent examination of brain science by Tim Hicks in his book *Embodied Conflict*, the author reminds us that cognitive biases afflict us all, mediators and users. For the latter, this is about the impact on decisions about entering mediation at all, as much as what happens during it. This topic is a field ripe for further discussion as we seek to frame the changes which will bring about much greater use of this hugely beneficial and constructive contribution to society which we call mediation. For providing stimulus and provocation along the way, Anna Howard deserves our gratitude and admiration.

Originally published in Kluwer Mediation Blog on 28 January 2021

Reflections on Mediation in Practice and Bringing Parties Together

It's been a long time since I wrote a blog just about mediation practice. Other things always seem more important!

However, as I was mediating this week, a thought occurred to me about a rather imperceptible but very real change in my practice as a mediator, which I develop here, albeit in a simplified way.

When I was initially trained, I learned the classic formula for mediation: straight into a joint meeting, opening "statements", then on to a series of private sessions (or "caucuses", to me a rather horrible word imported from elsewhere) with the parties, with the mediator shuttling back and forth between rooms. Parties might meet again but only rarely. So much then depended on the mediator's communication skills and how the mediator conveyed whatever information parties agreed to share.

There was a significant load on the mediator and it was heroic work in a way, leading to claims that the mediator achieved "success" by assisting parties to achieve resolution.

"I settled x% this year". All very mediator-centric and this possibly played to the pioneering spirit of so many of us who were keen to show that this new way of doing things was valuable and should be adopted more widely. And perhaps we felt that only we knew how to demonstrate the way it should work.

It also meant that the mediator could end up carrying the burden of "failure" when a mediation did not result in settlement. What did the mediator do or fail to do that led to that outcome?

I recall being sceptical when some colleague would tell of extended opening joint meetings and letting parties, clients and lawyers, continue talking about the issues even if things got a bit rough. I felt instinctively uncomfortable with that approach and could not see its value. Far better carefully to control the meetings and keep parties from further antagonising each other and risking a breakdown in the negotiations. I could not understand why some mediators followed the teaching of

Gary Friedman and others who, as I understood it, championed only meeting together, without private sessions.

Well, this week, I was surprised to take a step back towards the end of a mediation day and appreciate that a very large part of the event had taken place in joint meetings. Rarely did I carry substantive messages or information between rooms. It seemed far better to encourage the parties, whether the lawyers and/ or the clients, to do so directly by bringing them together to talk to each other. In that way, there was no risk of mixed messaging, of me confusing things, of laying the wrong emphasis on a particular piece of information, of misunderstanding a complex technical issue (about which they would always know more), of inadvertent breaches of confidentiality or indeed of slowing down the momentum by being too cautious.

It felt quite a change. I discussed it with my assistant who reminded me that I now bring years of experience and acquired intuition to what I do. That is true of course. Things which seemed clunky in the past happen more easily now. Conscious incompetence has given way to conscious competence and perhaps to unconscious competence. Perhaps. The risk with unconscious competence is of course how easily one can slip right back into unconscious incompetence. Apparent mastery becomes ineptitude, undergirded by complacency and even laziness.

My assistant reminded me of what we had actually done to set up the possibility of so much work being done jointly. There was a constructive tone throughout and everyone treated everyone else with dignity and respect. That wasn't accidental. We had all met in advance to discuss what the dispute was all about and to make sure effective preparatory steps were put in place. Communication continued by email in the build-up, with occasional phone calls. It wasn't all plain sailing however and apparently vital documents were still not available before the mediation day.

I had met privately with each team at the start of the day, always much more instructive than one expects in that, whatever has been set out in summaries and other papers in advance, the oral communication conveys more depth and nuance than had come across in writing. I had been able to pass on encouraging messages about intent and commitment in these early meetings. I find that early engagement of the key decision-makers, often meeting privately with me without lawyers present (always having discussed this with the lawyers of course) helps to build a constructive platform. It is, after all, their day.

Then each party had laid out its present thinking (not a mere repetition of summaries: I eschew the adversarial expression "position papers") but with a break after each had spoken to give the other party time to reflect, digest and absorb before framing their own articulation of how they see things (not a rebuttal or denial, I like to say). The breaks for consideration, which I often think might seem unnecessary, invariably and perhaps inevitably take longer than expected as people begin to see a different picture emerging from the preconceived ideas they may have (these days, I nearly always say a little about confirmation bias, reactive devaluation and other cognitive "traps").

And in those breaks, I join parties at some stage, make a few observations about what might be helpful, with a few gentle coaching suggestions, and those involved are usually keen to run their thinking past me. In these ways,

the risks of inflammation when parties meet is reduced significantly. I feel under less pressure and so my own tone is more relaxed and supportive, often laced with a bit of humour and chat about topics unrelated to the dispute but, I discover in the margins, of interest to those in the room.

I try to create a situation where the parties (hopefully the principal decision-makers) meet to reach final agreement. This reaffirms their sense of agency and is particularly important if there is any form of continuing relationship.

Reflecting on all of this, the reality is that I have innovated on the classic format with which I and many others were trained. But I suspect that few of us do things that way now anyway. There is still plenty of time spent in private rooms as parties chat about what to do next and how to do it. However, they spend more time together (in various combinations) and my role is even more that of choreographer rather than shuttle diplomat. I must say I enjoy that more and have a real sense of extending greater autonomy to the parties which, for me, is the primary purpose of mediation.

A caveat: each matter is different and there will still be cases where, for whatever reason, people may never meet or when the timing and frequency of such meetings, if they do occur, needs very careful thought. Horses for courses.

Finally, I'd like to dedicate this blog to my friend Stephen O'Rourke QC, a Scottish advocate and occasional mediator who was inspired by Gary Friedman and who died far too young, in tragic circumstances. He and his openness to new ways of doing things will be much missed.

Originally published in Kluwer Mediation Blog on 28 May 2022

Finally, in this section, this is a recent piece looking for a home...

Tiny Margins Make All the Difference

It was probably no more than a couple of centimetres offline. Nevertheless, the disappointment was palpable. Tiger Woods' putt on the 7th green in the first round of the recent Open Golf Championship at St Andrews slipped past the hole. As part of the watching crowd, it was a privilege for me to see this sporting great for possibly one last time. But this moment was also a reminder of the narrow margins between success and failure. Indeed, a fellow spectator informed us that someone had calculated that such a missed putt would cost several thousand pounds; increasing exponentially as the championship reached its later stages.

That same weekend, Scotland lost a rugby match (and a whole series) against Argentina in the final seconds of the game. Stuart Hogg, the resting Scotland captain, commented on television that *"tiny margins are the difference between winning and losing a Test match"*. Tiny bits of skill execution had let the Scots down, he said.

That got me thinking about professional practice and the tiny bits of skill execution that make all the difference in our work. It is easy in a busy world to lose the discipline to attend to detail, to check the small print, to spend the extra time on preparation, to stop and pause for a second or two before responding to an email. And yet focus and precision are essential in most of what we do.

It could be in expressing ourselves clearly and succinctly in a letter; that takes time and effort. Words attributed to Mark Twain come to mind: *"I didn't have time to write a short letter, so I wrote a long one instead."* It could be in the formulation of a question in a client interview or in the court room examination of a witness. Each word should be carefully chosen for its task, as was once said. Or in deciding whether to ask a question at all.

I recall an occasion as junior counsel, when I was in practice at the Bar many years ago, on which I acted for a third party in a claim about an accident at work. I listened to the evidence led on behalf of the pursuer and defender. Having undertaken careful preparation regarding the case against the third party, I elected to ask only one question in the course of three or four days of evidence. There was no need to do more; to do so would only put the third party in jeopardy. Less was more and self-discipline was essential. To the consternation of the defender, the third party was absolved.

Silence is golden, as the song goes. Sometimes, saying nothing and just waiting and watching is the best plan. As a mediator, I remember sitting for what seemed like several minutes resisting the strong urge to intervene as the two commercial leads in a dispute made proposals and counter proposals to each other. I could help most by staying quiet. Such inaction again requires self-discipline and a keen awareness of the dynamics of the situation. Inaction is not always appropriate of course and often the role of the mediator is to ask the one question that nobody else feels able to ask. You have to assess what is best each time.

That takes me back to preparation, for which there is no substitute. I recall the extent of preparation carried out by some of the senior counsel to whom I had the privilege of being junior counsel in my early days at the Bar. Yes, they were often very intelligent people but what marked them out was the hours and hours of preparation, anticipating every possibility, as one might in a game of chess.

The winner of the Open Golf Championship, Cameron Smith, was described as having a Zen-like mastery of his putting. The night before his sensational final round, he was apparently out on the practice green sending ball after ball towards the hole from different angles and lengths. That's commitment. And that's what it takes. In a different context, a recent obituary of the renowned theatre director Peter Brook noted that, for him, "everything depended on rehearsals". It won't always work but, in the long run, practice and preparation creates the master.

Fine margins are everywhere. One word, one question, a moment's pause. In your work this week, what might you do which will make the difference?

Originally published in The Scotsman on 1 August 2022

The Climate Emergency – and Mediation

As I mentioned in the Introduction to this book, the existential threat posed by climate change is very real and has exercised my mind considerably in recent times. The following pieces narrate a journey some of us have taken to try to make a small difference.

The World Mediators Alliance on Climate Change?

"The ground is so wet; it wasn't like this in the past. We can't get started on this year's soil preparation."

In a recent mediation involving farmers, this was the response to my early inquiry about how things were going, generally. These days, I find that the topic of climate change and its effects arises, incidentally, quite often in mediations across a whole range of topics.

Last week, I attended a seminar addressed by the chair of the UK Health Alliance on Climate Change. The UKHACC brings together doctors, nurses and other health professionals to advocate for responses to climate change that protect and promote public health. It coordinates action, provides leadership and helps amplify the voices of doctors, nurses and other healthcare professionals across the UK. The chair was both articulate and forthright about the risks we all face, the effects on healthcare and the opportunities for health care professionals to do things differently to help mitigate the impact.

That got me thinking. Many of us have argued for years that mediation

and encouraging interest-based negotiation is a demonstration of a sustainable, efficient, cost-effective alternative to an otherwise energy-consuming, expensive, carbon intensive process we call litigation. In many ways, mediation is a classic example of finding a better way to use scarce resources which would otherwise be diverted to less purposeful activity, helping to reduce unnecessary cost, saving time and labour, building more enduring, creative outcomes and renewing what might otherwise be dissipated energy. In other words, traditional zero sum, adversarial, win/lose paradigms are bad for the planet, while mediation fits into the model of environmentally friendly options.

If these propositions are broadly correct, what might that mean for mediators and our own practices?

Well, it suggests we can even more confidently promote what we do in the context of what will need to be rapid and wide-ranging changes to the way people do business. We can help in the initial stages of deal-making and alliance building, throughout the duration of projects and contracts in our role as conflict management specialists and, of course, down the line if and when disputes arise and need to be addressed quickly and effectively. This may only be achieved with a step change in what we do and how we do it, a quantitative shift in how and when we are utilised.

Secondly, it may mean that we need to consider how we go about what we do. Recently, I was invited to speak in Brussels about Mediation and Climate Change (for the full text, see the first volume of A Mediator's Musings). I can fly from Edinburgh to Brussels in just over 90 minutes. That would have been the preferable way to travel if I wanted to maximise my time to do other things before the event at which I was speaking. However, I chose to go by train, which involved a five-hour journey to London on the evening before, an overnight stay in London and catching an early morning Eurostar train to Brussels, another journey of nearly two hours. This meant that I had to plan my time differently and could not try to pack in an additional piece of work on the preceding day.

We are deeply committed to our calling. Many of us try to do a lot each week. But what are the implications for our mode of travel? What effect does it have on our carbon footprint? Might we mediators need to think about these things, such as the frequency of, and how we get to and from, our mediations? Is there someone more local who could do the job? And what about other aspects of what we do? Does everybody who attends mediation need to be there? Do we need to have folders of papers in hard copy form? Or could we all survive with only electronic transmission of documents? Probably? Perhaps many of us do so already.

We regularly travel far to attend conferences. How sustainable is that? What are the alternatives? How can we optimise our use of such travel as we do undertake?

I appreciate that this leads us to consideration of online dispute resolution and conferencing. Clearly that has a huge role to play as we seek to reduce travel and time spent. However, I was impressed recently to read about the contrast in the brain's responses to online socialising and physical meeting. The comparison was made between the addictive dopamine hit you get from a social media connection and the rich stew of oxytocin, prolactin and endorphins provoked by "real, actual human contact" (see The Changing Mind by Daniel Levitin). There will often be no substitute for meeting in a physical location. Perhaps, at least, what I am exploring here is about how to make those occasions when mediation is best done face to face as environmentally friendly as possible.

So, to wrap up: anyone for a World Mediators Alliance on Climate Change? WoMACC has a ring to it. To mirror the UKHACC, WoMACC would advocate for responses to climate change that protect and promote environmentally friendly dispute management and resolution. It would coordinate action, provide leadership and help amplify the voices of mediators across the globe. It would be our contribution to humanity's survival and thriving.

Originally published in Kluwer Mediation Blog on 28 February 2020

The Mediators' Green Pledge

Co-authored with Dr Anna Howard (Centre for Commercial Law Studies, Queen Mary University of London) and Ian Macduff (NZ Centre for ICT Law & School of Law, Auckland University)

"Homo sapiens, the wise human being, must now learn from its mistakes and live up to its name. We who are alive today have the formidable task of making sure that our species does so." David Attenborough, A Life on Our Planet

Looking back at John Sturrock's post from February which suggested a World Mediators Alliance on Climate Change, we are struck by how it seems to address a different era. Shortly after that piece was published, the coronavirus pandemic swept across the world bringing immeasurable loss and suffering. It also brought, for many, a heightened awareness of our interconnectedness with our planet and our impact upon it. It has also changed our mediation practices in ways we could not have foreseen just a few months ago.

As a mediation community, we have often talked about how we might mediate climate change issues. Perhaps we have not given the same amount of attention to how we might reduce the environmental impact of our own behaviour and practices as mediators – and in particular to how

we can individually and collectively play our part in reducing carbon emissions. The changes precipitated by the Covid pandemic have accelerated our ability to do so.

The movement to mediation using online platforms in response to the restrictions on face-to-face meeting imposed by the pandemic has, unexpectedly for many of us, shown us that environmentally-friendly ways of mediation can be both easily accessible and effective. That is not to deny that mediation in this way may bring particular challenges, many of which have been addressed by others and we will need to continue to refine our practices for the online setting during the continuing pandemic.

After the pandemic passes, while for some parties and some disputes face-to-face mediation may be the only appropriate option, for many others online mediation may well become the default option. Thus, the greater acceptance of mediation using online platforms has become an opportunity to make a meaningful reduction to the environmental impact of our mediation practices, something to which many of us believe we need to aspire in any event. Had the pandemic not occurred, we would still have wished to find ways to do so.

In response to John's open invitation back in February to create a World Mediators Alliance on Climate Change (WoMACC), members of the international mediation community came together to form a working group, with members from New Zealand, Germany, Scotland, England and Belgium. Over the past six months, the working group has explored what WoMACC could offer to encourage mediators individually and collectively to lessen their environmental footprint.

The main output is the Mediators' Green Pledge. This has been inspired by Lucy Greenwood's Green Pledge for arbitration and, with Lucy's kind permission, the working group has adapted that pledge for mediation. The Pledge, which was launched on 21st October, can be read on the special website (www.womacc. org) which has been created for this purpose. Already, signatures are being added daily.

While refining the Pledge, we had many intricate and lively discussions on its wording. Does the Pledge ask too much or too little? Is it sensitive to differences across countries and cultures? Might it demonise certain aspects of mediation which many may hold dear? The Pledge is designed to be illustrative, and adaptable. While there will certainly be aspects which we have missed, the Pledge is hopefully broad enough to allow all those involved in mediation to consider how they can make changes to contribute to a greener way of mediating. The Pledge offers a foundation upon which mediators can build with their own measures tailored to their specific practices and preferences. Signatories are welcome to augment and modify the Pledge as they wish. We encourage you to sign it.

It is easy to feel paralysed by the enormity of the formidable task identified by Attenborough. Can we really make a difference? Are those differences too difficult and too inconvenient to make? As Attenborough reminds us *"the truth is that we must do these things to save ourselves."* With that reminder, the changes we must make may suddenly appear more manageable. And perhaps they might also seem more manageable if we come together to commit to make the changes collectively, learning from and supporting one another.

The Pledge offers one way for us to come together to do so. As one signatory of the Pledge has said "*This pledge is a commitment that has no end and whether it is formalised or just remains a contract to myself – it feels really good to have begun it. Thank you for giving me the nudge!*"

We hope many others in the mediation community will feel the nudge!

Originally published in Kluwer Mediation Blog on 26 October 2020

Mediators' Green Pledge will form Foundation of Sector's Response to Climate Change

Recently, two representatives of the Law Society of Scotland wrote about the role of lawyers when it comes to climate change. They noted the crucial United Nations COP26 conference in Glasgow, now rescheduled for November 2021. The authors referred to lawyers managing their own environmental impact at work without expanding fully on what that might actually mean.

Last week, mediators around the world launched an initiative to address just that issue, with the Mediators' Green Pledge. We noted that mediation is a sustainable, efficient, cost-effective way to resolve disputes and other differences. As a mediation community, we also noted that we have talked about how we might mediate climate change issues. However, we recognised that we have probably not spent the same amount of time talking about how, as a community, we might address climate change in our own behaviour and practices.

We concluded that the time has come to address our contribution to the climate emergency facing us all. The move many of us have made to online mediation in response to the pandemic has shown us that environmentally-friendly ways of mediating can be both easily accessible and highly effective. The Green Pledge outlines concrete steps that each mediator can take, both during and after the pandemic, to reduce the impact upon the climate of each mediation we conduct.

As I write this, already well over 100 mediators from over 30 countries in every part of the world have subscribed to the Pledge, indicating their support for an initiative which could significantly influence the way in which we conduct many mediations. The Pledge is a broad foundation upon which, we hope, mediators will build with their own further measures tailored to their practices. Each case is different of course and flexibility is important, as in every mediation process.

The Pledge's wording could be useful as the legal profession considers what it might do:

"As a mediator committed to ensuring that I minimise the impact on the environment of every mediation I am involved in, I will ensure that, wherever possible:

- If screen sharing/video technology is appropriate, accessible and acceptable to all concerned, I will encourage its use in all aspects of my mediation practice;

- At all times during the mediation process, I will consider the most environmentally friendly way to travel if travel is necessary;

- I will offset the carbon emissions of any flights I make to and from mediations while recognising that this is not in any way a substitute for avoiding flying and will only fly when it is necessary to do so;

- At all times during the mediation process I will only correspond through electronic means, unless hard copy correspondence is expressly required in the circumstances, while recognising that electronic communication itself is carbon emitting and should be limited to what is necessary;

- I will not request hard copies of documents to be provided to me unless there is a special need to do so and I will discourage the use of hard copy documents generally;

- I will encourage parties and their advisers to consider the necessity of participants attending mediation in person if that attendance involves significant travel and is not necessary;

- Wherever possible, I will encourage parties and their advisers to consider the most environmentally friendly venue for their mediation. At mediation venues, in rooms in which I am mediating I will encourage, wherever possible, an environmentally friendly approach to the use of consumables (for example the avoidance of single-use plastic) and the use of energy (for example reviewing the level of air conditioning and heating);

- I will consider the appropriateness of travelling to, and my mode of travel to and from, conferences and other events and wherever possible will encourage and use live streaming/remote participation options;

- I will take steps to reduce the environmental impact of my office/workplace; and I will seek to raise awareness of this pledge, for example by referring to it on my website and/or email footer."

As one supporter wrote: *"This pledge is a commitment that has no end and whether it is formalised or just remains a contract to myself, it feels really good to have begun it. Thank you for giving me the nudge!"*

Originally published in The Scotsman on 2 November 2020

A Net Zero Civil Justice System?

Some time ago, I proposed establishing the World Mediators' Alliance on Climate Change. Out of that initiative grew the Mediators' Green Pledge. Out of that we hope to see a supportive corporate pledge and a conference at the time of COP26 in November. More on that later.

This month, I'd like to float another idea and seek comments and suggestions from readers. Here is where I have got to so far, written in the context of my own country, Scotland, but, I hope, adaptable to other jurisdictions:

CO_2 concentration in the atmosphere is at record levels, higher than for tens of millions of years. According to the former Governor of the Bank of England, and now UN special envoy on climate action and finance, Mark Carney, the world is on track for a 3 degree increase in warming. However, levels must be maintained at below a 2 degree increase if we are to avoid very serious damage to the world's environment and to our individual and collective futures. The world faces tipping points such as disintegration of ice sheets, species extinction and permafrost loss which could push parts of the earth into irreversible

changes. Feedback loops which will exacerbate adverse conditions are now a serious risk.

There is increasingly strong scientific and political consensus. The financial sector is beginning to understand the long-term consequences for investment and risk. As President Biden made clear recently, this is the decade when things must change and this is the year when we must start to make a real difference. Whatever we all do in response to the Covid pandemic needs also to address the implications of climate change and focus on achieving net zero carbon emissions as soon as possible. There is no time to waste. The Green Recovery needs to mean something. And to deliver.

The next Conference of the Parties on climate change, COP 26, will take place in Glasgow this November. Arguably, it is one of the most important global meetings ever. Nations now need to commit to implementing what was agreed at a previous COP in Paris. Overall, we are told that this commitment has been woefully insufficient so far.

Whoever we are and however we go about our lives, we all have a part to play in this, as Scotland's Climate Assembly recently reminded us. We have no choice. The UK Committee on Climate Change has challenged us all in Scotland to walk the talk. The Scottish Government has committed to reducing emissions by 75% by 2030. Experts say that we need to translate big picture commitments into sectoral delivery and real results on the ground, and to do so quickly.

My question is this: How can we design a civil justice system in Scotland fit for the future, not only post-Covid but addressing climate change and minimising environmental harm? How can we build a Net Zero Carbon Civil Justice System in and for Scotland? With COP26 coming up, how can we show leadership to other nations?

This raises some interesting questions:

- *What does or will the Law Society of Scotland recommend to its members to achieve an environmentally sustainable approach to helping clients to resolve disputes?*

- *What further can members of the Scottish Bar do to reduce fossil fuel emissions?*

- *How can the Scottish Courts and Tribunal Service do more with its online services to make a difference?*

- *What encouragement might judges individually and collectively give to litigants?*

- *What pledges or commitments might individuals and institutions in the civil justice system give to achieve Net Zero outcomes?*

- *How can we, in the civil justice system, engage with, involve and gain the support of the general public in a cooperative effort to produce tangible results?*

- *How can we frame creatively the discussions and decisions today and from now on to reflect the urgency of the situation?*

- *What might we learn from other civil justice systems in their response to climate change?*

- *In practice, what might all of this mean for patterns of consumption, use of renewables, travel and forms of process?*

The Master of the Rolls, Sir Geoffrey Voss, recently set out radical proposals for an effective and efficient civil justice system in England and Wales, including online integration of alternatives such as mediation, leading to, he argues, significant economic benefits for the country. The objective for the Scottish civil justice system must surely be to move from traditional resource-heavy processes to those which achieve the twin benefits of efficient dispute resolution and a lower carbon footprint.

'This is not for us...' won't do. We're all in this together. Those of us in mainstream professional activities in Scotland, including the civil justice system, must act now.

What do you think?

So, that's the general idea. What do readers think? Are there other angles? Better ways of expressing things? How could this work in your country? We know that mediation can be at the heart of a more sustainable civil justice system everywhere. What more can mediators say without appearing simply to promote mediation and facing the 'They would say that, wouldn't they?' response?

Originally published in Kluwer Mediation Blog on 29 April 2021.

Excerpt from a Keynote Address at the London International Disputes Week

"..we invite you to bring with you a reusable bottle to make use of the water fountains at the venue, although this is not a specific requirement."

Well done to the organisers of this event for making this notice so prominent in your pre-event information email!

Perhaps this needs to be a specific requirement: "No entry without a reusable bottle"! I have been asking myself: what can I add to the challenges which have already been presented to you?

Well, in true mediator style, perhaps what I can do is to ask some further questions:

- *How seriously do you really treat this topic?*

- *What has been your reaction – honestly – to what you have just heard?*

- *Do you view this as optional? Not for you? A bit irritating perhaps? Uncomfortable even? Perhaps not worthy of a keynote?*

- *Where does all this lead you – really? What does being sustainable and ethical mean – to you?*

- *For example, given what we have heard, should we each be capping the number of flights we take in a year – drastically?*

- *What other changes must we make to really address this?*

- *What would be the implications – really – for you, your clients and your practice?*

- *If we assume that the facts and the science – indeed the urgency - are now clear – and they are – why would we not make changes? Because of our business model? Our clients' expectations? Our sense of who we are? Our reluctance to change?*

- *Where would **not** changing leave us – and others – as we contemplate sustainability and ethics?*

- *If not us – you, me – then who? It is, after all, people like us who need to change what we do.*

Let's pause for a moment and ask ourselves the serious question: aside from reusable bottles, what else do we need to change – in order to make a real difference?

This takes me to mediation and the World Mediators Alliance on Climate Change (WoMACC). We now have over 600 signatories from over 50 countries around the world, with 15 or so translations.

Perhaps, in catching up with the other pledges, the Mediators' Green Pledge is a little like mediation generally: while mediation has a pedigree going back over the ages, it has only really come to prominence in recent times.

And that takes me to my major substantive point. While I respect both arbitration and litigation (after all, I practised for a number of years at the Scottish Bar), I suggest that mediation offers a distinctive way to reduce carbon emissions in many disputes.

I believe that our collective aspiration should be to achieve net zero carbon civil justice systems and net zero carbon dispute resolution overall. Anyone here who has been involved in mediation knows that, compared to most litigation and most arbitration, mediation is relatively quick, often more efficient, less time-consuming and less-resource intensive. Or it should be.

And mediation provides a useful route to identifying the underlying issues – what's really going on - and exploring a variety of commercial and non-legal options. Arguably and I acknowledge provocatively, mediation offers an even more sustainable means of resolving disputes, of achieving net zero– a greener form of dispute resolution if you like. And it seems to work really well online too.

Back to the Pledge. It all sounds great in theory but, again, what does it mean in practice?

It probably means sacrifice as well as commitment; on a personal level, I have lost the opportunity to act as a mediator in a number of cases by adhering until recently to an online policy when understandably some people want to meet in person; I have not been inside an aircraft for 26 months – that's hard as it means for example that I am missing an important mediators conference in Canada.

This is much easier for me at this stage in my career of course, and I do recognise the danger of being seen as too evangelical ...This is not easy stuff.

So, I come back to that email about the reusable bottle. Perhaps it really does need to be a specific requirement that we all bring one to an event like this – and that is just the start.

In Edinburgh, there is an exciting multi-media exhibition on the work of the artist, Vincent Van Gogh. He once said something along these lines: *"Great things are done by a series of small steps brought together"*.

Let's all pledge to take those steps now - and do great things together. We have no choice.

Delivered at Central Hall, Westminster, London on 10 May 2022

Reflections on the Mediators' Green Pledge: Where Are We Now?

Back in 2020, just before the world changed, I wrote a blog post suggesting the establishment of the World Mediators' Alliance on Climate Change.

My argument was that mediation offers a much more sustainable way to resolve disputes than many other processes. We could also do a lot to reduce our carbon footprint even if we maintained an in-person approach to mediation.

Then the pandemic came. The focus shifted and many of us discovered Zoom and other platforms. Mediating online became necessary and workable, indeed better than many of us could have imagined. I wrote about my own discovery of Zoom as a "revelation".

Out of this radical change in practice emerged the Mediators' Green Pledge and its associated website, about which Anna Howard, Ian Macduff and I have written elsewhere.

We noted that the Pledge *"offers a foundation upon which mediators can build with their own measures tailored to their specific practices and preferences."* We also recalled some of David

Attenborough's words: *"the truth is that we must do these things to save ourselves."*

I followed up with this question: *"How can we design a civil justice system ... fit for the future, not only post-Covid but addressing climate change and minimising environmental harm? How can we build a Net Zero Carbon Civil Justice System..."*

Where are we now?

That we are facing an environmental catastrophe is unarguable. Our species is presented with an existential threat. As the distinguished climate scientist, Katharine Hayhoe, says: *"...we are not adapting fast enough to the changes we've already seen, and if we don't cut our emissions as much as possible, as soon as possible, we will not be able to adapt."* And yet, as we know so well, our default setting when facing something incomprehensible is to slip into denial: "It's not happening...it's not going to affect us..."; or a feeling of futility: "there's nothing I can do... anything I do is of so little significance that..."

Against this background, it is interesting to reflect on the Mediators'

Green Pledge in mid-2022. As it approaches 650 signatories from all parts of the world, with many supporting organisations, what impact is it having and how are its signatories applying it?

It's not easy. There is an understandable demand for in-person mediation as we try to return to "normal". People are taking flights again as they did before. Mediators who try to persuade parties to mediate using an online platform may find that they lose work. The pressure to respond to client demand is strong. At least, we can take other steps to make a difference by insisting on transmission of electronic documents only. And we can try to make a point about heating, air-conditioning and other consumables at the mediation venue. But being loyal to the Pledge may cost us – or we may need to proceed in little incremental steps and hope that the message gets across somehow.

It can be awkward. At a recent mediation, the decision-maker on one side asked me about my flygskam lapel badge (a reminder of our need to reduce our air travel). It turned out that he owns two private aircraft for personal pleasure.

Most recently, I have been intrigued by the correspondence following a conference held by an organisation of which I am a member and which I had the privilege to address (via Zoom) on the topic of the Mediators' Green Pledge. At the conference, several participants caught Covid. Subsequently, there has been much commentary on the implications of the virus for such meetings. However, attempts to widen the conversation to include discussion of the appropriateness of travelling vast distances to such an event (and the virtue of online, alongside or instead) feel difficult. Indeed, one emerging theme may be that collegiality and personal meetings trump environmental concerns.

It's not easy. We need to talk about these things, and that means using good mediator strategies like finding what we have in common, what we agree on, and then exploring the issues and concerns that we all have. Indeed, if we can't do this, who can?

For me, aware of my own weaknesses and the charge of hypocrisy, there is a growing recognition of the moral dimension: a relatively small percentage of the global population in recent generations (me and others like me) has enjoyed the benefits of unrestricted travel with all the pleasure and benefits it brings. Many of us wish to continue to do so for that reason. However, our doing so is likely to play a part in creating a situation where the next generations will not be able to enjoy these and other things. Indeed, many of our fellow human beings are already suffering grievously – for example, we are told that up to 18 million people in Africa may face starvation this year in part due to climate change. Katharine Hayhoe sums this up: *"...the impacts of climate change fall disproportionately on the poorest and most vulnerable people. The 3.5 billion poorest in the world have produced 7% of heat-trapping gas emissions, yet they're bearing the brunt of the impacts."*

We now know all this. Arguably, if those of us who can afford to do so continue with our habitual lifestyles, we risk depriving our children and grand-children of their futures. I struggle to get my head round it all. Could it be argued that this is the ultimate in selfishness and self-indulgence? That is, for me, what makes this an ethical issue. It's not easy.

This takes me back to the role of the Mediators' Green Pledge. Our small organising group sometimes wonders if it is all worth it. But we are inspired by words like these from Katharine Hayhoe: *"That's how the world changes: When individuals have the courage of their convictions and use their voices to call for change"*. We have no other option.

Originally published in Kluwer Mediation Blog on 28 June 2022

The War in Ukraine - and Peace-Making

It is interesting — and extremely sad - to consider how the following pieces reflected some initial optimism (naivety?) before the war started and on how things have changed and deteriorated since then.

Warm, Respectful Talks May
Thaw the Threat of Kremlin

What is the risk that the Ukraine situation is being approached by the West in a binary, dualist way? We cannot control President Putin but how we, or at least our politicians and diplomats, respond will influence him. By binary or dualist, I mean adopting inflexible, black or white, right and wrong thinking.

This may result from seeing the Russians, or rather their leader, as an "enemy". It may lead us to perceive his strategy as purely aggressive, necessitating a similar response. The trouble with this, as we see, is that matters can become more inflamed, the threat of force can escalate and, crucially, there is less room for backing down or saving face.

The latter is likely to be important to the Russian leader. But there could be a danger that, by our own actions, we might create the very situation (invasion/war) that we say we wish to avoid. Paradoxes abound. It is of course possible that the West's strategy is to provoke Putin into acting — or retreating in humiliation. Long term, it is not clear that either would lead to greater stability.

What might be done? It is possible to engage constructively with your antagonist while still expressing your own position clearly and robustly. It's all about how you do it. First, the astute negotiator can acknowledge the perspective of the other, accepting that they see things differently. That is obviously true in this case. As viewed from Moscow, Ukraine presents a strategic risk to Russia. We do not need to agree with that proposition to recognise that Russians may feel vulnerable if their nearest neighbour elects to join the defence pact of its adversaries. Think of Cuba, Mexico or Canada joining the erstwhile Warsaw Pact.

Next, the negotiator can offer reassurances that they wish to work this out in a sensible way, addressing the concerns of all those involved. (Let us hope this is what's happening behind closed doors — it is exactly what happened in the Edinburgh Conversations in the early 1980s, which helped to end the Cold War.)

Throughout, we can engage and maintain respectful communication with Russia and all others with a stake. Having acknowledged and recognised their concerns and viewpoint, we must describe clearly what matters to us, and why, setting clear parameters that underscore our interests, and explain what we can and cannot do.

No concessions for concessions' sake but a mature conversation designed to reduce fear and find a constructive solution. This is not weakness but strength, courage and leadership. What is the alternative?

Originally published in The Times on 9 February 2022

The Situation in Ukraine – What Role for Mediation?

The escalating situation in Ukraine brings challenges to those of us committed to mediation and peace-making. Is there a time when what we stand for does not work and cannot be pursued? When dialogue, even in the most threatening of situations, is not appropriate? I don't pretend to have the answers but I have been reflecting on three very different examples of dialogue in the face of seemingly awful situations. What, if any, parallels or lessons might we draw? As you read what follows, what thoughts occur as we consider the Ukrainian situation?

The first example is the deeply personal engagement between Jo Berry, daughter of the murdered British MP, Sir Anthony Berry, who died when the Irish Republican Army attempted to blow up Britain's senior political leadership in 1984, and the man who planted the bomb which killed him, Patrick Magee. For more than twenty years they have met, initially courtesy of an intermediary, and talked privately and publicly about what happened and why.

Most recently, in an event to record that journey, they each talked about the need to listen and understand how the other saw things. Magee says that the Republicans in Ireland felt demonised, censored, not understood and silenced. He also now accepts that they demonised the enemy and couldn't see their humanity. Only in meeting Jo Berry could he discover that her father was a "fine human being". Only in meeting Patrick Magee, could she understand the oppression and breach of human rights which he experienced. *"I didn't meet him to change him but to see him as a human being,"* she explains. *"I'm really sorry I killed your dad,"* he says to her. Listening without judgement, they acknowledge each other's pain.

"Pain is the same everywhere, no matter the conflict," says Magee. Despite their differences and disagreements, they have been willing and able to sit down and have a conversation. They speak of rehumanising each other, rather than demonising. Berry asks herself what she would have done in his circumstances, in his shoes – what choices would she have made? They ask how each other's needs can be met knowing that, otherwise, there can be no sustainable peace. They talk about

changing the story, unlocking the narratives of the past, slowing down the dialogue, not simply trying to get their own message across or convert the other to a view of the world, but casting aside certainty and rightness and breaking things down to the level where they find they have so much in common. Berry commends a "cups of tea" policy to encourage respectful dialogue.

As Magee observes, if the resources in the world which are devoted to conflict were diverted to talking and finding common ground, we wouldn't have so much conflict.

A similar view about the excessive amounts spent on defence budgets (now, of course, being ramped up further as a result of the Ukraine situation) is expressed by the late Archbishop Desmond Tutu as he reflects on the work of the Truth and Reconciliation Commission in post-apartheid South Africa, in an interview with Tom Stipanowich of Pepperdine University.

We are different he says, not to be separate but to compliment each other and meet each other's needs. Everyone depends on everyone else – the African concept of Ubuntu where damage to you is damage to me. If I demonise you, I also demonise myself. Tutu reminds us that the enemy is also a human being, with their own fears

and expectations and moulded by circumstances. We need to connect.

This is all well and good, you might say, but where does all this leave us today? Well, my third example, which I adapt from my recent article in our national newspaper here in Scotland, offers some learning from the past. The escalating situation regarding Ukraine brings a chilling reminder of the days of the Cold War which came to an end at the beginning of the 1990s with the collapse of the Soviet Union.

My own country, Scotland, played an apparently significant role in the reduction of risk at that time. Throughout the 1980s, the University of Edinburgh played host to a series of private meetings, entitled the Edinburgh Conversations, with the theme of Survival in the Nuclear Age. These involved senior academics, military officials and diplomats from the United States, the Soviet Union and the UK, with no official status.

The Conversations alternated between Edinburgh and Moscow. Scottish location, informality and hospitality were at the heart of the events and I still recall the privilege of being a fly on the wall in Abden House in Edinburgh as the participants gathered for the start of one of the Conversations.

The meetings came about because the Professor of Defence Studies at the University, John Erickson, was a world-renowned expert on Soviet military affairs whose independence and creative genius meant that he was equally respected in the Pentagon and the Kremlin. That academic rigour and independence was critical.

On one occasion, the talks were due to commence in Edinburgh just a few days after Soviet jets had shot down a South Korean jumbo jet with 269 passengers on board.

Despite Western hostility, the talks proceeded, with everyone recognising the gravity of the situation and the importance of continuing to talk and prevent further escalation. The same approach was taken when the US launched an airstrike on Libya at almost exactly the time that another set of Conversations commenced.

When the talks began, East-West relations were arguably at an all-time low. Diplomacy was at a standstill. By their end, it was thought that the Conversations had contributed significantly to the transition in the Soviet Union. It was understood that neither side wished nuclear war. A modicum of trust had been built up. Personal relationships were established across ideologies. Frank exchanges had taken place. Presidents Reagan and Gorbachev had met in

Iceland and the dismantling of some nuclear weapons had begun.

The key must have been that people listened to each other, trying to understand the other viewpoint, recognising their needs and fears, with respect and courtesy, while being clear and realistic about what mattered to them. Judgments were suspended, at least in part, as they addressed the narratives of the past, humanising each other; indeed, as I recall, they would often find their common humanity in the course of shared social occasions, with cups of tea and more (often accompanied by music and gifts), which honoured traditions and offered moments of humour and relaxation – and opportunities to reflect intimately in private. Frustrations were managed and words would be detoxified and reframed when the talks looked like they might break down. Golden bridges were built, painstakingly, and victory speeches carefully crafted in the form of communiques, often taking hours during the night.

The Scottish hosts effectively worked as mediators, the third siders, and I remember the extraordinary efforts of my wise mentor, the late Michael Westcott, who acted as Secretary to the Conversations. He served in a wholly humble and authentic way, without ego, courageously giving his all, never seeking any personal approval or acclaim. His preparation, perseverance and attention to detail was immense. What an example.

Could something like this happen again? Whatever occurs in the short term, and assuming that we do not engage in mutual destruction, history suggests that dialogue will be needed at some point in the future, perhaps sooner rather than later. Attempts at mutual understanding, identification of real interests, hopes and threats, reduction of risk, better relationships – all are likely to have importance.

The key back in the 1980's was the presence of people of substance who brought to the Edinburgh Conversations their international reputations, skills and wisdom. We need to hope that people of this standing can be found somewhere in the world in 2022 and beyond.

As those of us who are mediators, third siders and peacemakers reflect on all of this, what might be our role today? As Desmond Tutu encouraged us: *"Do your little bit of good where you are; it's those little bits of good put together that overwhelm the world."*

Originally published in Kluwer Mediation Blog on 28 February 2022.

A version of this, focussing on the Edinburgh Conversations, was also published in The Scotsman on 23 February 2022

Difficult Tasks Ahead for Peacemakers

As a mediator, and therefore as someone predisposed to peace-making, the situation in Ukraine is deeply troubling. Is there a time when peace-making is redundant? We must hope not. The alternative seems too awful to contemplate.

But what might peace-making entail? I offer some thoughts here, but with a caveat. Some of this may not be so easy to contemplate given all that is occurring.

Firstly, peacemakers would suggest we separate people from the problem. Here, that probably means acknowledging that the major protagonist is not the Russian people but the regime in the Kremlin and its leader. We can direct our disapproval towards President Putin and his supporters but endeavour to continue to treat ordinary Russian folk with respect, while recognising many of them have no access to objective reporting.

Peacemakers would emphasise the need to be careful with language. Using words which unnecessarily inflame the situation may not be in our interests; it takes self-discipline to be clear and frank in what we say without descending to provocation and insults.

Perhaps that is why some people have been concerned about President Biden's unscripted asides. There is a balance to be struck of course...

We know the temptation to respond angrily comes from our fight and flight survival instincts, crucial in prehistoric times but prone to cause error now.

Generally, peacemakers will want to engage what Noble laureate Daniel Kahneman calls "system 2 thinking": measured, thoughtful, rational thought processes, especially when under pressure and even if that approach is not reciprocated.

Pausing and taking time to reframe key messages is likely to be important. Off-the-cuff remarks can be damaging.

That doesn't mean that we resort to soft soap, far from it, but peacemakers need to find an approach which has our underlying needs and interests at heart. To do this, further steps may be necessary: William Ury, of Getting to Yes fame, would urge us to "go to the balcony" and survey the big picture. Thinking medium to long term, what is most important to us? For example, despite the pressure of the current conflict, we cannot forget the existential threat of climate change.

What effect might that have on the peacemakers' negotiating strategy? We see that coming into play as we consider energy supplies. Again, where does the balance lie?

Peacemakers are helped by considering what in the jargon are known as BATNAS and WATNAS – our Best and Worst Alternatives to a Negotiated Agreement. These require a realistic assessment of what will happen if some sort of agreed resolution is not achieved. In other words, if we don't reach agreement, what's the best we can anticipate will happen? And also the worst? These can be tough to face, especially if we don't like where it takes us. However, with nuclear and chemical weapons potentially in play, these techniques provide peacemakers with a useful reality check, a benchmark for decisions.

If we aspire to a peaceful outcome, those involved can't avoid undertaking this kind of risk analysis, much though they might wish not to. While bystanders may say "don't compromise after all you have been through", they are not in the firing-line and often don't face the hard choices which benchmarking like this entails.

A difficult but often necessary task is to get into the shoes of those we dislike most. That may be essential if peacemakers are to get past the zero-sum nightmare. What might it be like to be the person we fear most? What is really going on in their minds? What can we do to influence their thinking? What do we need to change to bring about the outcome we seek? What, if any, concessions might be made to get what we need? How important might it be to enable the other to save face? Who are the unseen constituencies for whom "victory speeches" might need to be written, that enable the opponent to say that they have achieved enough?

Interestingly, these are probably all questions which faced President Kennedy during the Cuban missile crisis 60 years ago and to which, by all accounts, he responded courageously and with self-discipline.

So much for the theory. The real question is: how are Ukrainian and other negotiators approaching this? Certainly, viewed from afar, President Zelensky seems to have a good grasp of negotiation essentials. We must wish all the peacemakers well.

Originally published in The Scotsman on 11 April 2022

Ruling out Peace Talks with Russia could be a Mistake

Stewart McDonald MP (SNP Defence Spokesperson) describes the horrors experienced in Ukraine and articulates well the concerns felt there about any change in the West's position, prompted by "extreme voices from the left and the right across Europe".

He writes that "one cannot negotiate a lasting peace with Putin". While it is not clear whether this extends to Russia generally, Mr McDonald is clear that Russia must not be allowed to win the war.

If one accepts the latter proposition, is it necessarily the case that negotiation can never occur? Let's accept that no concessions should be made that reward Russia's actions or are inconsistent with what Ukrainians wish. Where does that leave the West? Expecting surrender? Encouraging total victory? How likely is that to happen? What would be the consequences of trying to achieve it?

There are countless examples from history where negotiation has taken place with those who were sworn enemies: the IRA, the apartheid regime, the Taliban, for example.

By contrast, in the Second World War, Winston Churchill concluded that Germany must be defeated absolutely. Which position do we take now? How do we make wise decisions?

Perhaps, rather than approaching this in a binary way, we must accept the reality of complexity and contradictions. It is perfectly possible to argue for and maintain your principles, self-respect and objectives, while also seeking to end conflict. The key is to be clear about your and others' long-term interests.

It is not an indication of weakness to seek to understand what motivates the other party, the enemy; indeed, that can be a sign of confidence and strength. Understanding is not the same as conceding, appeasing or legitimising.

Nelson Mandela's biographer Richard Stengel writes: "This way of thinking is demanding. Even if we remain wedded to our point of view, it requires us to put ourselves in the shoes of those with whom we disagree … But the reward … is something that can fairly be described as wisdom."

Perhaps we should never negotiate with the Russian leadership. But if one argues for such a position, it is important to articulate clearly the risks inherent in alternative courses of action. Emotional or intuitive responses are not enough.

There are risks in negotiating of course. This week's news may appear to make it less likely that there can be a negotiated solution with Russia and its leadership sometime in the future. However, it could be a strategic error to exclude the possibility altogether.

Originally published in The Times on 22 September 2022

Dear President Putin...a Thought Experiment

I have been musing about what a mediator might say to President Putin given the opportunity. That led me to compose a letter a few weeks ago, with which I have since tinkered. This is merely a thought experiment. The letter goes something like this:

"Dear President Putin

I write as a mediator, a peacemaker. I do so in the hope that there may still be a constructive way to bring an end to the tragic situation in Ukraine.

[*note to self: Would PP see this as "tragic"? What other starting lines might such a letter need in order to engage him?*]

To do so, my experience tells me that people who disagree with you need to try to understand better what motivates you. That would help them to identify what, if anything, they can do to help bring about a speedy conclusion. I accept that you see the world differently from others, especially those in the West. We know from what we have heard that you and others look on with concern at some of what you see in the West. And I acknowledge that Russia has experienced many episodes of aggression towards it in its history. I

recognise also that Russia is a proud country.

[*note to self: Would this sort of acceptance, acknowledgement and recognition work with a person like PP? Does he feel he has not been heard?*]

I am interested in you. If I may, I have some questions for you. What happened to you, way back, when you were much younger? What experiences have shaped you as a person? What was it like for you growing up? What happened in your family? Who did you love, back then? Who loved you? What about now? Who do you love now? What are they thinking about you now? What do you think of them? Does any of this matter to you? Do you care? How easy is it for you to talk about any of this stuff?

[*note to self: We know that we are all shaped by events in our past; but would any of this work with someone like PP? Is it naïve to think that these sorts of questions have any utility? But don't we need to try to get under the surface if we are ever to find a way forward that is not violent? Let's keep going:*]

What do you really think about what is happening now? In your heart of hearts? What do you fear most? What do you fear losing? Who do you fear? Why does it seem that you need to control everything around you? What are you fighting against, inside? What do you regret most of all? What and who do you wish to protect? People, places, things, hopes, dreams? From what? What lies behind your mask? How, if at all, do you challenge yourself and your thinking? If you're stuck, how can you get yourself out of this? What would release you from all this, if anything? Can you even contemplate these questions? If you can't, where do you end up?

[note to self: Some of these questions might be perceived as judgemental or aggressive. Would we feel that we could ask robust questions? If we did, what effect would they have? As mediators, how do we create an environment where we can ask these kinds of questions? What would it take to achieve that here, if anything?]

You – and others – may think this foolish. Please don't mistake this letter. I am not suggesting there is an easy solution, nor that people will accede to your wishes. In fact, we need to recognise that there are strong views on all sides. Achieving peace is hard work, involving hard labour. But the alternative is hard too, for you as well as for others.

[note to self: Could we get into a BATNAS and WATNAS* conversation? Does PP

do that kind of thinking? And then some more tough questions:]

What would get you out of this that others can deliver? Who do you need to persuade or impress? What do they need? What options have you – and others – not yet explored? Medium to long term, what can be done to get us all to a different place? With that in mind, do you worry about climate change? I recognise that the transition to a non-carbon future world-wide must be a difficult prospect for Russia, given your reliance on the sale of fossil fuels to support your economy. What might others do to help? Could that make a difference?

[note to self: Is there something we are all missing? Going to the precipice and then to the balcony, what might we see that we haven't seen before?]

President, I don't know if you listen to music at all. There is a singer/writer, now deceased, call Leonard Cohen. I am not a big fan of his music but he has this lyric: "There is a crack, a crack in everything. That's how the light gets in." Can we, somehow, find that crack here?"

[note to self: How do you finish a letter like this? What would be an attention grabber? Or is this just sentimental guff? And, worse still, offensive to those who have suffered so much?]

So, there it is. As I say this is merely a thought experiment. Make of it what you will. In conclusion, I am grateful to my friend and colleague in the Mediators' Green Pledge coordinating group, Sabine Koenig who, in another context, today sent these words: "For more than ten years I have been carrying now in my purse Ken Cloke's quote: *"Every conflict reflects what each person most needs to learn at that moment."* Right now it seems that I may need to learn a lot more." We all do, Sabine. We all do.

Originally published in Kluwer Mediation Blog on 28 April 2022

*BATNAS and WATNAS are the negotiator's jargon for "Best Alternative to a Negotiated Agreement" and "Worst..."

Back in July 2017, when the world was a different place, I was fortunate to visit Moscow and St Petersburg. Some of what I wrote in a blog post then resonates now:

Knowing our Neighbours – a Mediator's Reflection

I am travelling back from a couple of days in and around Dublin, discussing an initiative on respectful political dialogue with politicians, academics and conflict resolution professionals. It was a privilege to spend time at Glencree, the centre for peace and reconciliation which was one of those places where so much was done in recent times (and is still being done) behind the scenes to ease the conflict between communities in Northern Ireland and the Republic of Ireland.

I was struck by a remark made by one of my hosts to the effect that most people in the Republic of Ireland knew very little about their neighbours in the north. This is on an island which covers about 32,000 square miles (a bit less than the size of Indiana) and where the distance from Dublin to Belfast is about 100 miles.

Two weeks earlier I had visited Moscow and St Petersburg for the first time. This trip to Russia was nothing less than a revelation. How little I knew about that great country, which spans nine time zones and has a land mass greater than the surface area of the planet Pluto. The traditions, the culture, the ethnicity, the language, the economics and, most of all, the geography. A country which has been invaded countless times in its history, suffering extraordinary losses, not least the over 20 million deaths sustained in World War 2. A country whose western and south western borders are with nations which were once a part of the Soviet monolith but are now viewed as satellites of a West which in turn is seen, perhaps unsurprisingly, as unfriendly. (It was interesting to learn that, for many Russians, "Ukraine" means "borderlands" of Russia). However tangible is the threat, the feeling of insecurity seems very real.

None of this may justify some of the Russian government's contemporary actions. But it does help one to understand them better and to be thoughtful about what steps are most likely to ease tensions.

Separately, Russian youngsters in these cities have, we learned, very similar aspirations to those of our own: a good job, an opportunity to better themselves and to benefit from modern life. They experience too the frustration of property values well beyond their means. In the hinterland, it seems like life may be similar to that in the US hinterland. Shades of *Hillbilly Elegy* by American writer and politician, JD Vance. Indeed, our very seasoned Moscovian guide pondered that the Russian psyche may be much more like that of America than we dare imagine.

How little we know about each other. How much we are prepared to assume however. And how easily we are led to judgements. These tendencies seem detrimental to building sustainable relationships which will enable us to survive and thrive, whoever and wherever we are. The same applies, of course, to the commercial disputes in which many of us now participate as mediators.

How little the disputants often really know about each other: their financial situations, the problems of supply chains, the failures of sub-contractors, the effect of a change in senior staff, the discovery of an unforeseen physical problem with a project, the limitations of technology, the frailties of human nature. Contracts are designed of course to circumvent many of these imponderables. But we all know how expensive, time consuming and destructive a contractual dispute can become and how important getting under the surface to the real issues can be. That is where, even late in the day, a good mediator can add real value.

A good mediator will look for ways to enable people to get to know each other and understand more about how they really see things. I often invite all concerned to have breakfast together. That allows them to mingle: lawyers, experts, clients and support teams. After a few words from me, the principal decision-makers often stay behind for an informal chat together with me. How revealing that can be, how helpful to the establishment of a working relationship which can pay dividends later. In some matters, that moment can be cathartic, tough, difficult, uneasy, a revelation. The point is that it has the possibility of beginning the kind of change in tone which may be essential to move matters forward. And to enable those involved to find out what is really going on, what it is really about. What lies under the surface?

How much more might be done if we could reverse engineer some of our disputes and encourage business and individuals to consider and understand, at the contract/ relationship-creation stage, some of the human and other non-legal or even non-commercial factors affecting their counterparts. More robust and sustainable deals might be done. Much cost and angst might be avoided. We might even hope that international diplomacy and foreign affairs would (re?)turn more to such an approach in the dangerous years ahead, rather than seeming to perpetuate stereotypes and often poorly founded mythology.

Funnily enough, I have just been reading the private memoirs of my mentor, Michael Westcott, who, a generation ago, was Secretary to the Edinburgh Conversations, a series of tripartite confidential meetings between military, academic and political experts from the USSR, the USA and the UK, which have been credited with helping to ease relations at the height of the then Cold War. I had the privilege to attend one of these in 1983. Just one anecdote: in the first meeting in Edinburgh, sessions took place in an informal lounge setting with easy chairs, no formal agenda, and good food and Scottish entertainment. The reciprocal meeting that year in Moscow was initiated in a very formal room with representatives of the delegations ranged opposite each other across a large table. On the crucial matter of seating arrangements, it took much skill by my mentor to find an acceptable compromise with his Russian hosts which would enable the conviviality of Edinburgh to be regained.

Just as in Glencree in the Republic of Ireland and Corrymeela in Northern Ireland, so much was achieved just by finding a seating arrangement which encouraged sworn enemies to talk. And to find out that they had much more in common than ever separated them. In those talks, they agreed that using nuclear weapons against each other was unthinkable. A similar thought crossed my mind as I watched young folk enjoying an early evening drink in St Petersburg. Just like our own young people.

We return to the oft-asked question: Who is our neighbour? What do we really know about him/her/them? How much might we gain by really trying to get to know them? What do we need to do about it?

The Scottish poet **Iain Crichton Smith** writes in "**Neighbour**":

Build me a bridge over the stream
to my neighbour's house
where he is standing in dungarees
in the fresh morning.

O ring of snowdrops
spread wherever you want
and you also blackbird
sing across the fences.

My neighbour, if the rain falls on you,
let it fall on me also
from the same black cloud
that does not recognise gates.

Printed in Great Britain
by Amazon